·SOLDIERS OF ROME·

·SOLDIERS OF ROME·

PRÆTORIANS AND LEGIONNAIRES

ROBERT F·EVANS

Line drawings by
KATHARINE EVANS

Seven Locks Press
Publishers
Cabin John, Md./Washington, D.C.

Library of Congress Cataloging-in-Publication Data

Evans, Robert F. (Robert French), 1910-
    Soldiers of Rome.

    Bibliography: p.
    Includes index.
    1. Rome. Army—History. 2. Rome—History, Military.
I. Title.
U35.E92 1985   355'.00937   85-26230
ISBN 0-932020-36-4

Typographic design and maps by Dan Thomas
Jacket design by Lynn Springer
Mezzotints on pages 75 and 76 adapted from photographs,
    National Buildings Record, Great Britain.
Printed by Thomson-Shore, Inc., Dexter, Michigan
Manufactured in the United States of America
First edition, February 1986

Seven Locks Press
Publishers
P.O. Box 72
Cabin John, Md. 20818
202/362-4714

Acknowledgments ———————————————————————

    The author is indebted to a number of friends who have helped in the preparation of this study. Giles Constable, professor of history at Harvard, Hunter Rawlings, head of the classics department and vice chancellor of the University of Colorado at Boulder, and John Headly, professor of history at the University of North Carolina at Chapel Hill, have read the first draft and made numerous improvements in the text. Maxwell Davenport Taylor, General, U.S.A. (Ret.), corrected a number of errors and suggested several views that had not occurred to the author. Charles Collingwood, Burke Wilkinson, novelist and biographer, and Robert Amory, former counsel of the National Gallery of Art, were kind enough to review the text and make a number of important suggestions.

RFE

To Jane

Foreword

by Edward B. Atkeson
Major General USA (Ret.)

In the late eighteenth century, Edward Gibbon wrote in his monumental *Decline and Fall of the Roman Empire*, "The arms of the republic, sometimes vanquished in battle, always victorious in war, advanced with rapid steps to the Euphrates, the Danube, the Rhine and the Ocean; and the images of gold, or silver, or brass, that might serve to represent the nations and their kings, were successively broken by the *iron* monarchy of Rome." The iron was borne and wielded under the empire by the soldiers of the legions and of the praetorian guard. These men constituted the world's first standing army—regularly recruited, governed by regulation, and drilled to conform to standard tactics on the battlefield.

Wherever in the known world the troops might find themselves, they would draw up their camps in a square with their eagle, or legion standard, at the center. They were organized and equipped in conformance with uniform tables, consumed authorized rations (which they often supplemented on their own) and upon reaching their twentieth (or so) year of service, were retired with ceremony and a handsome gratuity. Their professionalism was a wonder in a world largely given to rudimentary socialization and tribalism. For five hundred years these soldiers held an empire together and influenced the course of history to the present day.

But there was a darker side to their nature as well. Just as they kept—or imposed—the order of empire, they often helped shape—and sometimes imposed—the political leadership

General Atkeson is a former deputy chief of staff for U.S. Army, Europe.

of the state. Emperors had reason to be concerned about the mood of the troops in the barracks. Gibbon wrote of Augustus, "How precarious was his own authority over men whom he had taught to violate every social duty! He had heard their seditious clamours; he dreaded their calmer moments of reflection." Even Tiberius spoke of exercising control of the army as being like holding a wolf by the ears. While military professionalism attained high art among the troops of Rome—especially among the centurions, the company commanders—it did not include the modern Western concept of apoliticism. The praetorian guard, and to a lesser extent the legions in the provinces, were frequently the effective selectors and deposers—usually by the sword—of emperors. Certainly no one could rule the state without the backing of the army.

The reader will discover remarkable parallels between the armies of the caesars and those which he has come to know in the modern world in his own time. Organized as the emperor's guard, the praetorian troops on occasion revealed some of the characteristics and tendencies more recently associated with such elite formations as the *Waffen SS* of Nazi Germany. Generally the praetorians were better armed, better trained, and more politically conscious than their brothers in the regular forces. Oddly enough, however, they seldom seem to possess the fierce intensity of loyalty to their leaders that twentieth-century observers found among the ranks in Hitler's *Leibstandarte*. At times it seems that the praetorians' services were available to the highest bidder.

Lest the stain of mercenariness color the modern view of Roman troops too deeply, it should be recognized that the praetorians frequently made important contributions to the development of the provinces and to the maintenance of stability and peace. When they were not engaged in the pursuit of the seemingly interminable wars, the legions constructed roads and walls, bridges and canals. One is reminded of the similar role played centuries later in the New World by U.S. Army engineers. As this republic set out to find its way in its environment, these engineers were beset at times by fierce and hostile tribes who had little more sympathy for or understanding of the concept of manifest destiny than the tribes of Germani had for the glory of Rome.

Soldiers of Rome is history; especially it is the story of military professionalism two thousand years ago. But, as with so much history, it has a great deal to say to us today. The reader will understand how the image of "the man on horseback" has held such fascination for peoples and has been the subject for such extensive debate for centuries since. The principal institution that enabled Rome to extend its power over millions of square miles, from Britain to the Middle East, and to hold that power for half a millennium, will be forever a model and a basis for comparison of all military organizations. Colonel Evans is to be congratulated for bringing us this important work.

Contents

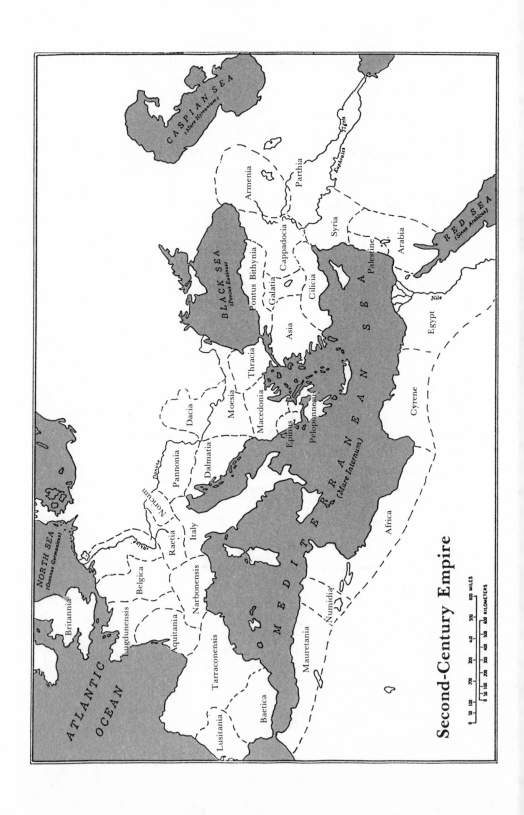

Second-Century Empire

Author's Preface

During the first three centuries of our era, the Roman Empire was the most powerful political entity in the Western world. The superb army that protected and expanded the empire had three parts—the legions with about 150,000 men, the auxiliary with another 150,000, and the praetorian guard, which had at its peak about 10,000. Both the legions and the guard were made up, at least in theory, of Roman citizens. The auxiliary consisted of non-citizens who were paid about half as much as the men of the legions. The guardsmen, on the other hand, were elite troops and were paid much more than the legionnaires.

This study devotes itself to the guard and the legions. Part One is a history of the guard and Part Two an order-of-battle study of the legions. Much of Part Two was published in 1980 in a limited edition.

***

"The evil that men do lives after them; the good is oft interred with their bones."[1] So it has been with the praetorian guard. The historians of the classical world had a distinct dislike for the guard and gave it a bad press. With this volume the author hopes to give a more balanced picture.

The study that follows owes much to Dio, Herodian, Tacitus, Plutarch, and whoever wrote the *Augustan History*. Modern commentaries have been freely consulted, as noted in the bibliography. The guard itself heretofore has not been the subject of a history; to write this one, I have in the main stitched together incidents variously reported by the classical authors in their accounts of related events.

After the days of Augustus, Rome had three power centers. First was the senate, which exercised legislative and judicial power and normally selected the emperors. Second was the emperor, who in theory was first among equals in the senate but who in fact ruled as a dictator. The third power was the praetorian guard, an organization of a rather conservative nature that did not condone stupid emperors and took a particularly dim view of those, like Nero and Elagabalus, who were exceptionally and publicly licentious. It was the custom for upcoming emperors to present themselves to the guard for acclamation, a ceremony that took place either before or after the senate voted the new emperor his powers.

The principal historians writing during the period of empire were men without military experience;* three of them were probably members of the senate. Moreover, these historians had a habit of sprinkling their accounts with letters and quotations from speeches made up from whole cloth, a convenient way of attributing to somebody else their own prejudices. Had Julius Caesar lived a hundred years later, we might have unbiased commentaries and more faithful portrayals of both praetorians and emperors. As it is, anyone attempting to build a history of the praetorians is left with sources notoriously lacking in objectivity. It appears that all who mention the praetorians have an ax to grind, and almost all are strongly biased against them— undoubtedly a reflection of both the writer's place in society and his aim in writing. Among the ancients, Tacitus had the scholar's contempt for, and fear of, the professional soldier; Dio saw praetorians almost exclusively as makers of emperors; Herodian tended to scorn them. Suetonius, a follower of Constantine, naturally reflected that emperor's hatred of the guard. These writers did not always agree, even about emperors. Tacitus called Vespasian's rule in Africa infamous and odious; Suetonius, on the other hand, said it was "upright and honorable."

---

* A conspicuous exception may have been Marcus Aurelius, who spent many of his nineteen years as emperor (A.D. 161-180) in the field and who is believed to have written an autobiography. Regrettably, the only work of his that has come down to us is his *Reflections* or *Meditations*, a marvelous contribution to philosophy but of virtually no value as history.

Besides their distrust of the praetorians, what these authors seem to have had most in common is an intense and disapproving interest in the sexual behavior of the emperors. Without a doubt, if less space in Roman history had been devoted to Eros and more to the military, this study would be more nearly complete. Nevertheless, by submitting existing sources to rigorous analysis, I have attempted to disentangle the praetorians from the attitudes, largely those of Rome's upper middle-class, and prurient interests of the ancient historians, as well as from the Victorian values that infest most of the modern commentaries. The effort, however, has been rather like preparing a history of the United States Army from accounts in *Commonweal*, the *New Republic*, *Playboy*, and the *National Enquirer*.

Fortunately, one does not find the same bias against the legions. This may result from the fact that the legions were not stationed in or near Rome itself and were considered to be a menace neither to the senate nor to the senatorial class.

The method used in preparing Part Two is that of the army intelligence service[2] rather than that of the scholar. It is, in effect, an order-of-battle study of Roman legions. Works of both ancient and modern scholars have been combed for references to specific legions, the references then being collated to produce histories of the individual legions. When conflicting reports turned up, and they often did, the most plausible was used without excessive review of the evidence. All works consulted are listed in the bibliography and are readily available. Historical evidence of the legions is plentiful for the first century and a half but sparse for the period 150-300. The reader will note a concentration of incidents before the year 150. Histories of legions formed after 200 are not included, as these legions did not, in general, conform to the pattern. They were often small organizations and "legions" in name only. Similarly, numbered but unnamed legions that did not survive beyond the year 10 are not listed. No effort at all has been made to record the history of auxiliary troops. The reader may assume that auxiliary cavalry and infantry units were attached to the legions in most combat situations.

With a modern atlas, the reader should be able to follow

the tracks of the legions without undue trouble. Geographical terms have been converted, where possible, to modern usage, on the assumption that most of us are poorly informed about first-century names for countries, provinces, and cities. St. Albans, for example, is used instead of Verulamium and Northern Turkey instead of Pontus.

Five maps are included in Part Two to show the distribution of the legions in 30, 80, 130, 180, and 230. The base of the flag staff of a legion indicates its location. When no staff is shown, the legion is understood to be in the general area, although its exact location cannot be determined. A sixth map is included to show the Roman names for provinces and other areas during the second century.

The line drawings of the emperors by Katharine Evans are, in general, based on numismatic portraits.

Robert F. Evans

Part One

The Praetorian Guard

prae-tó-ri-an Of, pertaining to, or designating the bodyguard of a Roman emperor....Resembling or characteristic of the praetorian soldiers, esp. as to corruption, political venality, etc....One who defends an established order, a conservative.

Webster's Second International

prae-tó-ri-an-ism The control of a society by force or fraud, esp. when exercised through titular officials and by a powerful minority.

American Heritage Dictionary

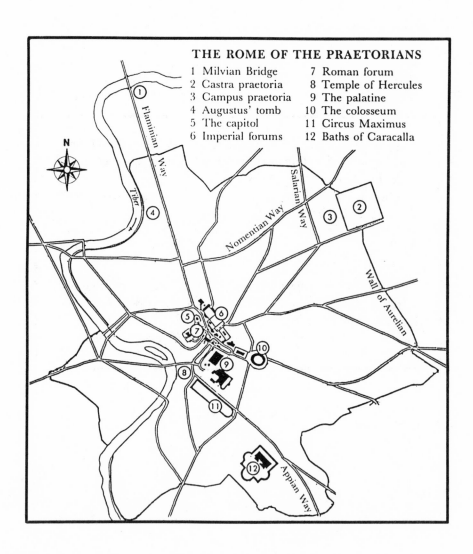

THE ROME OF THE PRAETORIANS

1 Milvian Bridge
2 Castra praetoria
3 Campus praetoria
4 Augustus' tomb
5 The capitol
6 Imperial forums
7 Roman forum
8 Temple of Hercules
9 The palatine
10 The colosseum
11 Circus Maximus
12 Baths of Caracalla

N

Flamminian Way
Tiber
Salarian Way
Nomentian Way
Wall of Aurelian
Appian Way

One

Germany and Cremona

The Roman Empire of the first centuries of our era included western Europe to the Rhine, North Africa, the Middle East, part of southern Russia, and the Balkans south of the Danube. The legions of Rome were on the perimeter, extending Roman power from Scotland in the north to Memphis and Baghdad in the south and from the Crimea and the Tigris in the east to Spain and Morocco in the west. Roman fleets controlled the North Sea and the eastern Atlantic as well as the Mediterranean, Black, and Red Seas. At the center of this power was the emperor and his praetorian guard. No legion was normally stationed in Italy, which was the province of the guard. Late in the period, a legion, II Parthica, was at Albano, but its five thousand men never challenged the preeminence of the ten thousand praetorians.

The emperor Augustus founded the guard about 27 B.C. Constantine destroyed it on 28 October 312, at the battle of Milvian Bridge. During the intervening 338 years the guard was a unique military and political force.

Augustus was one of the great military planners in history, the organizer of the first Roman regular army. Until his time, troops had been raised for specific campaigns and then demobilized at the close of those campaigns. By establishing a regular force, he was able to reduce the number of legions from sixty-odd to twenty-eight. He found that 140,000 regular soldiers, with a like number of lower-paid auxiliary troops, could secure the far borders of the empire. He set up the first war office, which paid the troops from two taxes initiated A.D. 6; a sales tax on auctions in Rome (one percent) and an inheritance tax (five percent). He also provided generous retirement benefits, including grants of land and money, as well as exemptions from

1

all taxation for the soldier and his wife for the rest of their lives.

When he established the regular army, Augustus also set up on a permanent basis the praetorian guard of nine cohorts. Men of the guard were organized, armed, and trained in a manner similar to those in the cohorts of the legions. The praetorians, however, were picked men of Italian origin. They were paid three times as much as soldiers in the legions and received retirement benefits after only sixteen years of service.

The word *praetor* has a long Roman history. Five centuries before Augustus it was the title of the commander of the army. It then evolved to become the title of a provincial governor with military powers. It was also used for centuries for magistrates in Rome and elsewhere. The quarters of a general in a military camp was known as the "praetorium," the principal gate to the camp "the porta praetoria," and the cohort that served as the general's guard "cohors praetoria."[1] The term was thus an obvious one to be used for the emperor's permanent guard.

Authorities differ as to whether the first cohorts of the guard were organized with five hundred or one thousand men each. Five hundred is the probable figure, but at the end of the second century one thousand was clearly the cohort strength. Although the guard's primary purpose was to protect the emperor, over the years this mission expanded to include administrative and judicial duties. The commander of the guard, the praetorian prefect, often served as commander-in-chief of the armed forces.

The cohorts of the guard, each under the command of a tribune, were made up of centuries—that is, units—of eighty men each, with a centurion in command. The centurions were the professional soldiers of experience advanced from the ranks in the legions. They were looked to for command in battle, and their noncombat duties included training. The tribunes, on the other hand, were not professional soldiers but men of the equestrian class. In the politico-military Roman world, serving as a tribune in the guard was one of the steps in advancement. Such men tended to alternate civilian and military service and often, after years as tribunes, went on to become provincial governors or commanders of a legion. Former centurions who finally achieved the rank of tribune in the guard rarely progressed to higher rank and usually retired after such an assignment.

Armament and equipment of the guard were similar to that of the legion. Each guardsman was outfitted with two seven-foot throwing spears, or *pila*, and a short sword. The spear, with a wooden shaft and a bendable metal point to prevent its reuse by an unhit enemy, was the basic weapon for the opening of an engagement. After the spear attack, the soldier used his two-foot double-edged sword as a thrusting, not a slashing, weapon. Barbarians slashed. Romans thrust.

For protection, the soldier had a metal helmet that early in the period was bronze, then iron. By the middle of the period the helmet was bronze again, but with an iron skullcap inserted. A fastener for the plume was on top, but plumes were worn mainly on ceremonial occasions. The shield was oblong, curved to the shape of the body, and made of a kind of plywood; it had a rawhide cover and a metal binding around the edges. At the center was an iron boss that, on the inside, provided the handle. The front of the shield was painted with the distinctive markings of the guard's cohort and century. Because of the size and importance of the shield, the sword was worn in a scabbard on the right side, rather than on the left as in more modern armies. Body armor consisted of overlapping metal strips protecting the chest and shoulders. Similar strips around the trunk were hinged in the back and held together with leather thongs. Although complicated and time-consuming in assembly, this armor provided freedom of movement as well as protection. Greaves (armor for the legs below the knees) were not usually worn as they would have impeded movement. The rather complicated leather military boot was provided with nails for more secure footing.

The standards of the cohorts, in a sense, took the place of the modern flag, being used extensively in ceremony as well as in combat. Great disgrace went with the loss of a standard to an enemy, for it was the totem of the cohort. The various symbols on the standard are not fully understood. There were animal totems, discs representing decorations, open hands, animal figures, zodiac signs, and, in the case of the praetorians, small portraits of the emperor. On ceremonial occasions, the standards were wreathed with garlands. In combat, they were used to signal orders to the troops. Praetorian standards were more complex than those of the legions and often were so heavy that on the march they had to be transported on muleback. Augustus was not unaware of the possible danger inherent in the maintenance of a large military force in Rome. While he was emperor, no more than three of the nine cohorts were ever in Rome at any one time; the other six maintained the peace in other towns and cities in Italy. For a time, three cohorts were as far away as Aquileia, near Trieste on the Gulf of Venice. Augustus rotated the cohorts in the spring and fall. With each cohort was a thirty-man squadron of cavalry that rotated with it.

Augustus took two other steps to ensure that the guard would not get out of hand. He provided that there should always be two praetorian prefects who would, in effect, keep an eye on each other. He also established the principle that the prefects would be drawn not from the most powerful class in Rome, the senatorial, but rather from the next order down, the equestrian. Some prefects were former *primi pili*, very senior centurions who had earned their equestrian rank through distinguished military performance.

Although Augustus introduced the idea of two mutually accountable prefects, he was also the first to depart from it. He appointed as joint prefects A.D. 2 Quintus Ostorius Scapula (subsequently prefect of Egypt) and Publius Salvius Aper. Later, though, he replaced these two with a single prefect, Valerius Ligur, and a few years after that appointed Lucius Seius Strabo to replace Ligur.

Interestingly, Augustus also established three cohorts of city troops who were paid considerably less than the guard but were commanded by a prefect of senatorial rank. If his intent was for the city troops to act as a counter-weight to the praetorians, he failed. The city cohorts performed their duties as city police over the coming three centuries but never seemed to have challenged the guard.

Despite all the precautions taken by Augustus, the guard

was to become involved in the selection of future emperors often in future years. Four of the praetorian prefects were themselves to become emperors.[2]

Two other agencies established by Augustus should be mentioned. The watch, some seven thousand strong and made up of seven cohorts, was set up A.D. 6 as the fire brigade of Rome. It also served as a paramilitary force and a reinforcement for regular troops in times of emergency. Finally, there came into being the *speculatores* under the command of the praetorian prefect. These men served as the emperors' couriers to and from the provinces and as special-mission agents when unpleasant tasks like killing suspected traitors had to be done. They also served as a secret police.

When Augustus died A.D. 14, Rome was racked with sorrow. His funeral pyre was lit by a praetorian centurion in accordance with a decree by the senate and into the fire guardsmen threw their proudest possessions—triumphal decorations earned for deeds of valor. At the reading of the emperor's will it was learned that he had bequeathed one thousand sesterces (ten gold pieces) to each guardsman, five hundred to each member of the city cohorts, and three hundred to each soldier in the legions. His personal finances were in such good shape that this tremendous bounty could be, and was, promptly paid.[3]

At the close of his life, Augustus had turned over more and more of his duties to his stepson, Tiberius Claudius Nero. When Augustus died, Tiberius was in all ways virtually emperor. It should be noted, however, that after the two consuls, the first to hail Tiberius was Lucius Seius Strabo, the praetorian prefect, which seems to have legitimatized the appointment without prior approval by the senate. *Speculatores* were sent to the governors and commanders with orders to have the troops swear allegiance. Soon thereafter Tiberius appointed as second prefect Strabo's son, Lucius Aelius Sejanus, who was to have a tremendous impact on the office.

The first important mission of the guard during the year 14 was to help put down an uprising of the legions in Pannonia (western Yugoslavia). Three legions—VIII Augustus, IX Hispana, and XV Apollinaris—were in summer camp together under the command of Quintus Junius Blaesus. Hearing the news of Augustus's death, the troops mutinied, demanding more pay and the right to retire after sixteen years like the praetorians. They beat some of the centurions badly and killed at least one, Lucilius, commonly called "Give-me-another" because of his habit of breaking vine-wands on the backs of recalcitrant soldiers. Finally, Blaesus gained time by agreeing to dispatch his son, a senior officer, to Rome to plead the cause of the soldiers. Detachments sent to Nauportus (present-day Vrhnika) for road building and bridge construction looted the city, then turned on Arfidienus Rufus, the tribune in charge, and marched him back to camp under a back-breaking load. Once back in camp, the troops fueled the mutiny further, among other things imprisoning Blaesus's household staff.

When news of the mutiny reached Rome, Tiberius sent his son Drusus to negotiate a settlement. With him went two reinforced cohorts of the guard with cavalry, possibly 250 troopers, all under the command of Sejanus, the newly appointed prefect. Approaching the camp of the three legions, Drusus was met not by a welcoming party but by groups of surly, ill-kempt soldiers. He had great difficulty making himself heard but somehow managed to propose that the demands for increased pay and earlier retirement be referred to the senate. His proposition was not well received. Why had *he* come to Pannonia, the men wanted to know, if the decision had to be made by the senate? The situation then began to get serious. The mutineers menaced the officers of the guard and one senior officer of Drusus's staff, surrounded by the rebellious troops, was stoned severely and rescued only at the last moment by a contingent of praetorians.

That night there was what appears to have been an eclipse of the moon. The soldiers took this as a bad omen and next day came around to a less violent position. Capitalizing on their fears and less belligerent mood, Drusus rounded up the ring-leaders, who were then executed either by their centurions or by the praetorians. There followed storms so violent that the men asked to be returned to their winter quarters. The revolt was over. The legions were sent back to permanent camps. With

Sejanus and the praetorian cohorts, Drusus returned to Rome.

A similar revolt broke out the same year in the Rhineland, where Germanicus, one of Rome's great generals, was in command. Germanicus was the nephew of Tiberius, brother of the future emperor Claudius, and father of another emperor, Caligula. At the time of the outbreak in the Rhineland, Germanicus was away in France supervising the collection of taxes.

The army of lower Germany led the revolt, and the four legions—XXI Rapax, V Alaudae, I Germanicus, and XX Valeria Victrix—made essentially the same demands as had the troops in Pannonia. Germanicus hurried back from France but before he arrived many of the centurions had been killed by their own men. Once he did arrive he was almost outshouted by the mob. Struggling to make himself heard, he first directed the soldiers to form into their units. They refused. He then ordered that the standards be brought forward so that he could at least know to whom he was talking. This the soldiers did reluctantly. After explaining the seriousness of their conduct, Germanicus promised in the emperor's name that they would be retired after twenty years' service and that the last four years would be light duty. He also promised to double the announced bequest from Augustus, making it six hundred sesterces per man. Grumbling, the men acquiesced and returned to their winter quarters.

At this time, Germanicus decided that an invasion of Germany would take up the slack in his legions and get the armies in better shape. The army of the upper Rhine, which included II Augusta, XVI Galica, and XIV Gemina, had not mutinied, but Germanicus saw that its soldiers got the same benefits as those in the army of lower Germany who had.

In addition to the two armies with their attached auxiliary troops, Germanicus, as a member of the imperial family, had two cohorts of the praetorian guard under his personal command. The campaign in Germany was launched A.D. 15 and lasted through the following year. It was at the close of this campaign that the two cohorts proved their particular worth.

Germanicus had swept through Germany as far as the Elbe and defeated or brushed aside all the tribes opposing him. On the return march, however, the Germans regrouped and tried to repeat their victory of six years earlier in the Teutoburgian woods, when Varus had three legions destroyed. Germanicus, though, was no Varus but a highly skilled general. His forces, withdrawing toward the Rhine in the vicinity of the Ems River, were heavily attacked. His march formation had placed the two guard cohorts in the center, the legions before and after them, with part of the auxiliary troops in advance and the other part in the rear. Usually, armor and weapons were carried separately. This time, anticipating the German action, Germanicus conducted the march with the troops fully armed and ready for combat.

When the Germans sprung their trap, the Roman columns wheeled in the open ground near the Ems and attacked in line of battle; Germanicus himself commanded the guard cohorts in the center. Great slaughter resulted, for the guard caught the Germans with their long spears and swords in the heavy woods where the shorter javelins and swords of the praetorians were far more effective. After several days of this slaughter, the Romans no longer had an enemy to fight. Germanicus sent some of the troops back to the Rhine overland while he, presumably with the guard and other troops, went by boat. A tremendous storm scattered the fleet, possibly causing more casualties than the Germans had.

Germanicus asked Tiberius for one more year to wipe out the last of the Germans, but Tiberius instead ordered him back to Rome. Tiberius was probably persuaded to do so by the prefect Sejanus, who was very jealous of Germanicus's successes and wanted no more of them. It was the wish of both Tiberius and Sejanus that only two cohorts of the guard go forth and welcome Germanicus to Rome, and only two were ordered. To almost nobody's surprise, however, seven cohorts marched out to greet him. Germanicus was not only the most successful of living Roman commanders but a man of great style, admired by soldiers and civilians alike.

In Italy, things had hardly been dull for those cohorts not involved in either the mutiny in Pannonia or the German war. During the first few years of Tiberius there were serious disorders in the theater in Rome; a centurion of the guard was killed and a prefect seriously wounded. In southern Italy, a former member of the guard, Titus Curtisius, started an uprising among slaves. Three patrol ships of the Roman navy put in to Brundusium—the center of the revolt—and initially slowed down Titus Curtisius. From Rome by forced marches came a strong force of the guard under the command of Tribune Staius that finally put down the rebellion, captured the ring-leaders, and returned to Rome with the prisoners.

A more unpleasant episode took place at Pollentia, a town in the northern foothills of the Apennines. Here the population held the corpse of a leading centurion until his heirs would agree to put on a free gladiator show. Tiberius dispatched one cohort from Rome and another from the western Alps to converge on the town. According to Suetonius, whose accuracy is questionable, the emperor required that the magistrates and most of the population be imprisoned for life. (One cannot help wondering who the jail keepers were.)

The most important development for the guard during the reign of Tiberius was its growing concentration in Rome on forty acres just outside the Porta Viminalis. Sejanus, who was now sole prefect,—his father having been made governor of Egypt—persuaded Tiberius that this concentration was in the best interest of the imperial family. From this time forward, the guard was a major influence on events in Rome.

Most authors attribute great ambition to Sejanus. Although not born of the senatorial class, he aspired to become emperor. He ingratiated himself with Tiberius and slowly sowed distrust of Germanicus and the emperor's son, Drusus, who stood in his way. His ambitions took a turn for the better when Germanicus, who in the year 17 had been appointed overall commander of the eastern provinces, died in Antioch, some say by poisoning. Gnaeus Piso, the imperial governor of Syria and theoretically under Germanicus's command, was accused of the death. Summoned to Rome, Piso was tried by the senate but committed suicide before a verdict could be reached. He had wrongly assumed that Sejanus would testify in his defense.

In the meantime, Agrippina, the widow of Germanicus,

returned A.D. 21 to Rome with the ashes of her husband. There was a great outpouring of emotion. When Agrippina came ashore, she was greeted by two cohorts of the guard as well as civic leaders from much of Italy. Drusus returned from Dalmatia. Only the emperor, who had developed a keen dislike for Agrippina, remained invisible. After Germanicus's ashes had been deposited in the mausoleum of Augustus, Drusus returned to the armies of Illyricum. Only he now remained to impede the advance of Sejanus. He died A.D. 23 of poisoning, a murder carried out by his wife but believed by many to have been arranged by Sejanus. Germanicus's two children, who might also have been impediments, were subsequently put to death—Nero in 20 and young Drusus in 33.

Tiberius continued for some years to put his faith in Sejanus. He praised him to all and had statues made of him as a great hero of Rome. To impress the senate with the might at his command, he had Sejanus put on a training drill of the guard for the senate to watch. Although he failed to follow through, he even told Sejanus that he would arrange a marriage for him within the imperial family.

The emperor spent the last eleven years of his life, 26 to 37, on the island of Capri—not returning to Rome during this entire period. His move from Rome was believed to have been instigated by Sejanus, who in his absence could exercise almost imperial power in Rome itself. Sejanus controlled virtually all communications between the government and the emperor, as the *speculatores* were the imperial message service. Aware that he was becoming more and more unpopular in Rome, Sejanus tried to ensure that nothing unfavorable about him would get to the emperor. He made regular trips to Capri to keep his image clean; on one occasion, when there was a rock slide and he put his body between the emperor and the falling rocks, he got credit for saving Tiberius's life. In 31 he was made consul, almost the highest honor the emperor could bestow.

Nevertheless, in time word got through to Tiberius that his praetorian prefect was plotting his overthrow, as indeed he was. Sejanus had learned that the emperor meant to name Caligula as his successor, and Sejanus felt that he would have to move fast to prevent it. Apparently, he also moved incautiously. Tiberius found out and decided Sejanus must go. Secretly the emperor made Naevius Sutorius Macro, a former commander of the watch, praetorian prefect and through him sent a message to Sejanus: Sejanus was to attend a meeting of the senate and receive a special honor. Working with Publius Graecinius Laco, then commander of the watch and an old friend, Macro arranged for a detachment to replace the normal praetorian guard at the temple of Apollo where the senate was meeting. There Sejanus was accused of seeking the emperor's death, convicted, imprisoned, and the same day executed. Macro had spent much of the day at the castra praetoria ensuring loyalty of the guard to him and the emperor.

The senate condemned, and ordered to be executed, both of Sejanus's children and many of his relatives and supporters. (Most of these committed suicide, for in Rome at this time those that killed themselves could pass on their estates to their families, while those who waited to be executed had their properties seized by the state.) Dio records, as an additional aftermath to Sejanus's execution, that the guard rioted, looted and burned houses—not, he says, out of love for Sejanus but to make it clear that any remaining friends of his were their enemies. Neither Tacitus nor Suetonius confirm Dio's account of the pillaging, and one tends to think that this charge is merely one more surfacing example of Dio's dislike for the praetorians. On the contrary, Rome appears to have been rather quiet these first days of the new year, with most people waiting to see how things would go with the new praetorian prefect.

Macro continued as the guard prefect for the remaining six years of Tiberius's life. As the emperor himself never came to Rome, Macro ran the affairs of empire as prime minister. Among these affairs was the matter of Pontius Pilate who, from the household of the emperor, had been appointed procurator in Jerusalem A.D. 26. Ten years later, Pilate was thought to have done a rather poor job and L. Vitellius, governor of Syria and brother of the future emperor, sent him back to Rome where presumably Macro found a less demanding job for him.

Tiberius showed generosity toward the guard and, during

Macro's time as prefect, gave large grants to the praetorians. When Tiberius finally died on 16 March 37, Marco was at his bedside. According to Tacitus, Macro became impatient at the slowness of his dying and helped him on his way by smothering him in his bedclothes.

History records that during Tiberius's reign only two important buildings were constructed in Rome: the temple of the god Augustus at the foot of the Palatine, and the great castra praetoria built in 21 and 22.

One of the first things that the 24-year-old Gaius Caesar, better known as Caligula, did on coming to power was to honor that part of Tiberius's will that gave three thousand sesterces to each member of the guard. To this, at a review and parade of the guard, he added one thousand sesterces of his own. Donatives of smaller size were given to the soldiers of the city cohorts and the legions in the field.

Caligula had a strong military background, being the son of Germanicus and having been born in one of the legion camps. As a child he was often with the troops, and his nickname, Caligula, came from the miniature army boots that he often wore with his child-size army uniform. His coming to power was popular with the army.

Historians have not been kind to Caligula, telling endless stories of his personal misbehavior. Reportedly, he had a number of spectators killed at the circus when they grumbled about his doings. He is also said to have wasted vast sums on showy but useless projects. One of these was the building of a bridge of ships three and a half miles long between Bauli and Puteoli, covering it with earth and planks and then leading the entire guard over it in a parade. Macro, it seems, was visibly less than enthusiastic about the emperor's conduct. Annoyed, in 38 Caligula appointed him prefect of Egypt, then disposed of him before he could take up his new duties, forcing him and his wife to commit suicide.

Having depleted the treasury and confiscated vast sums, Caligula undertook a campaign in Gaul in 39. He marched a few miles into Germany,—having crossed the Rhine—but then marched right back again with little or no contact with the Germans. He then proceeded with his forces, which must have included most of the guard, to the English Channel, where he seemed about to invade Britain. After boarding ship, he sailed off from shore and then sailed back again. The historians say that the troops were then required to gather sea shells to take back to Rome, where he entered with an ovation. His expedition was not entirely fruitless, however. He had executed a number of wealthy individuals in Gaul and confiscated their estates.

Some authors deduce that Caligula was at least partly insane. In Rome he resumed his strange conduct, executing people for no reason other than to get hold of their property. Finally, two tribunes of the guard decided to act, presumably with the approval of the prefects, Rufrius Crispinus and Sextus Afranius Burrus. One of the tribunes was P. G. Cassius Chaerea; the other was Cornelius Sabinus. To Chaerea, the emperor had been insulting, calling him a wench and, when he had guard duty at the palace, giving him watchwords like "Love" or "Venus." In January 41, the two tribunes intercepted Caligula in a narrow corridor outside a theater and killed him. Most of the population rejoiced at his death and praised the two tribunes. The senate was certainly pleased. It had both Caligula's wife and daughter executed.

Although all the authors are highly critical of Caligula, he did perform at least one far-sighted act for Rome during the less than four years he was emperor. He sent a centurion, one assumes from the guard, to Corinth to survey a canal across the isthmus.

After his murder, some of the praetorians went through the various rooms of the palace. In one, they found Caligula's uncle, Claudius, hiding behind a curtain. These guardsmen decided that Claudius should be the next emperor and carried him in a litter to the praetorian camp. Claudius resisted the idea, or at least made a good show of resisting, but the more he resisted the more the guard was determined to enthrone him. Meanwhile the senate debated who should be emperor and sent tribunes to tell Claudius not to accept. On arrival at the praetorian camp, however, the soldiers accompanying the tribunes promptly joined Claudius's supporters. Still resisting, the senate occupied the Forum using city troops, but soon capitulated when a crowd of citizens turned up in support of Claudius. On the day after Caligula's death, Claudius agreed to serve and the senate elected him.

One of Claudius's first acts was to give each member of the guard 150 gold pieces. Every year thereafter, on the anniversary of his coming to power, he gave each of the guards 100 sesterces. As a further expression of his indebtedness to the castra praetoria, he issued gold and silver coins commemorating the guard's oath of allegiance and depicting his admission to the castra.

As for the two tribunes who had killed Caligula, Claudius had Chaerea put to death, after which Sabinus killed himself. It was not for fondness of Caligula that Claudius had the two eliminated but, rather, to register his disapproval of the assassination of emperors.

One of the most important steps that Claudius took concerning the guard was to raise the number of cohorts from nine to ten. This further increased their influence on events.

Claudius, though an unattractive man personally, was an excellent administrator. Something of a scholar, he greatly improved the legal system and set up what amounted to a civil service. His foreign relations were well conducted and advanced the cause of Rome.

Claudius did, however, have trouble with his wives who, in turn, made trouble for the prefects. Valeria Messalina, his wife at the time of his accession, was much younger than he, strong-willed and resentful of opposition. The scholar Seneca, who had influence with her husband, was exiled to Corsica on her orders. She had the praetorian prefect Cantonius Justus killed when it appeared that he would inform Claudius of her various affairs. When she went too far in her unempress-like conduct, Claudius, who was away at Ostia, had the guard seize her friends. Returning to Rome, he was not sure whether she was mounting an insurrection, so he proceeded directly to the praetorian camp to ask whether he was still emperor. The troops, assuring him that he was, demanded that Messalina and her friends be punished. Messalina herself was killed when Narcissus, Claudius's freedman and head of his household staff, faked orders from the emperor to the praetorian tribune at the palace. Back at the castra, Claudius made a speech to the effect that he had been most unfortunate in his married life and had no intention of marrying again. This he forgot almost overnight.

All seemed to concur that Claudius should have another wife and the consensus was that it should be his niece, Agrippina, the daughter of the famous general Germanicus. She was another strong-willed young woman, intent on being an effective co-ruler. The senate highly approved and passed a special act authorizing Claudius to marry his niece, such marriages otherwise being illegal.

Agrippina almost immediately had trouble with the two prefects, Lucius Geta and Rufrius Crispinus. They were removed in 51 and her own selection, Sextus Afranius Burrus, made sole prefect. Geta, like his predecessor Macro, was made governor of Egypt, but unlike the unfortunate Macro was permitted to go there and assume his duties.

Agrippina was also pushing hard to have her own son by a previous marriage, Nero, set up to succeed Claudius. Seneca was called back from exile to be his tutor. Claudius's own son Britannicus was quietly eased out of the picture.

In October 54, Agrippina felt that the drift was away from her son. So, to make sure of Nero's succession, she killed Claudius by having him served a plate of poisonous mushrooms. Uncertain of the reaction from the praetorian guard, she kept Claudius's death a secret for several days. When she thought the time ripe, Nero was taken to the praetorian camp and there proclaimed emperor. The senate soon acquiesced.

Although unsuccessful in the handling of his wives, Claudius did have success in his one major war of aggression. His invasion and the conquest of most of Britain in 43 went off like clockwork. He himself was in Britain less than three weeks. He presided over one battle and returned to Rome to celebrate a triumph. Rufrius Pollio, who was joint prefect with Cantonius Justus, must have been the praetorian prefect in command of the guard cohorts in the British invasion, for he was awarded the right to be seated in the senate whenever the emperor was there. It seems, however, that he was executed later in Claudius's reign.

Also participating in the campaign in Britain was Marcus Vettius Valens, a soldier in Cohort VIII of the guard. According to an inscription honoring him found in Rimini, near San Marino, Valens received numerous decorations at that time and went on to be centurion in Cohort II and later tribune of Cohort III. His career peaked with service as *procurator* in Lusitania. A *procurator* was governor of a small province, or the chief finance officer of a large one, and rising to such heights from the ranks was rare.

Nero came to power on 13 October 54 at the age of sixteen. He had been groomed for the job. His stepfather Claudius had adopted him, and he was married to Claudius's daughter Octavia. Thanks to his tutor, Seneca, he was fluent in Greek and had made a number of speeches in Latin and Greek. As a grandson of Germanicus, he was popular with the people and seems to have had a wry sense of humor; on one occasion, referring to the manner of Claudius's death, he called mushrooms the food of the gods. Even before Claudius's death he had made a handsome gift to the guard and had led a ceremonial march by the praetorians with shield on arm.

After Nero was safely installed, a struggle developed for control of the young emperor. The praetorian prefect, Burrus, and his former teacher, Seneca, tried rather successfully to keep Agrippina from taking over the government herself. Nero was feeling his way. He relieved the guard from providing good order at the games but from subsequent rioting soon learned that he had to have a cohort present on those occasions.

The struggle between Burrus and Agrippina continued for several years, with the mother gradually losing ground. Nero did not enjoy being bossed by his mother and finally, in 55, sent her away. About the same time he set aside his wife Octavia and took the beautiful Sabina, wife of the former praetorian prefect, Rufrius Crispinus. Sabina is generally credited with talking Nero into killing Agrippina, which he did in 59. Nero used sailors to do the killing, for he was not sure that he could count on the guard to obey him. After the murder, hoping to ensure the guard's loyalty, he made another donative.

That same year, his fifth as emperor, Nero began to develop his personal interest in the theater and in performing. He used a large contingent from the guard as his claque when he gave his first lyre concert and had Burrus standing beside him. He also began to interest himself in the world at large and sent an element of the guard to Egypt with instructions to explore the sources of the Nile. He gave thought to the Caucasus as well. At the time of his death in 68, he was gathering troops for two campaigns, one to conquer Ethiopia and the other to capture the area north of the Caspian Sea.

The life that praetorian prefect Burrus led under Nero could not have been an easy one. Not only did he have to keep an eye on the emperor's activities but, in handling the jobs of commander-in-chief of the armies and foreign minister as well as national treasurer, he was very busy indeed. The war that broke out in 54 in Armenia, thanks to the intervention of Persia, required careful handling despite the fine work of a great Roman general, Corbulo. In 61, there was the war in Britain, caused by an initially successful revolt headed by Boudicca. When this war was finally concluded, a palace crisis developed when Sabina persuaded Nero to have Octavia killed. Sensing that Nero's standing with the guard would be seriously damaged by such an action, Burrus opposed it strongly but without success. Burrus died later that same year, some historians attributing his death to poisoning, presumably at Sabina's instigation. After Burrus's death, Seneca retired from the court, and the coast was clear for new favorites.

As prefects of the guard, Nero then appointed Faenius Rufus, a distinguished Roman, and Gaius Otonius Tigellinus, who seems to be best remembered as the most active participant in Nero's rather peculiar orgies. The two prefects did not think well of each other. Two years later came the great fire in Rome, when a large part of the city was destroyed. There seems to be no historical basis for the legend that Nero started and enjoyed the fire. It does seem true that he did a magnificent job rebuilding the city.

In the meantime, Nero was becoming more and more unpopular. Tigellinus had an influence just the opposite of Burrus's. The young emperor's violent and rather cruel nature was stimulated into a number of senseless killings and silly theatrical activities. In 65 a number of leading citizens organized a plot to dispose of him and to put in his stead G. Calpurnius Piso, a distinguished senator. Praetorian prefect Faenius Rufus was the leader, and a number of tribunes and centurions of the guard were involved. Tigellinus got word of the plan, reported it to Nero, and a blood bath followed. Piso committed suicide. Rufus, the guard tribunes and centurions, and many others were executed. Even Seneca, who according to most historians had nothing to do with the plot, was required to kill himself.

From this time on, Tigellinus was even closer to Nero. A second prefect was appointed to take the place of Rufus—a career soldier, Nymphidius Sabinus, who had served well in Pannonia. Sabinus, it appears, took over responsibility for all military functions of the guard, leaving the political to Tigellinus. Once the executions and replacements were done, Nero made a speech to the assembled guard and granted each a donative of two thousand sesterces, again hoping to buy loyalty. This effort, however, was hardly furthered by the hounding to death of many more people, one of whom, for reasons never made clear, was Rufrius Crispinus, who had been praetorian prefect under Claudius. Toward the senate, Nero became increasingly overbearing. Under his orders, two cohorts of the guard occupied the temple of Venus Gentrix, the senate meeting place, intimidating the members into condemning Clodius Thrasea Pactus, a leader of the republican minority, and numerous others.

The year 66 was a busy one for the guard. It had to put on a tremendous ceremony in Rome for the visit of the king of Armenia, Tiridates, who came there to be invested by Nero. After the investiture, much of the guard had to go to Greece with the emperor, who was appearing there in various dramatic competitions. While in Greece Nero revived the interest in a Corinth canal and directed the praetorians to get on with digging it, a project hardly calculated to endear him to the guard.

He himself dug and took away the first basketful of earth.

The guard was not alone in its disrespect for Nero. The senate obviously thought poorly of him for having killed so many senators. On his return to Rome, the emperor found the guard, the senate, and the populace seething with ill will. Military revolts broke out in Gaul and Spain. In June 68, sure of the guard's support, the senate declared Nero an enemy of the state, after which the guard left the palace and returned to the castra. Despite Nero's pleadings, none of them would go with him when he fled the capital. On the contrary, a mounted detachment of praetorians was sent after him. They found him in the home of one of his freedmen. When he heard the sound of horses approaching, he killed himself.

The years 68 and 69 were active ones for the praetorians and fatal ones for their prefects. The prefects, Sabinus and Tigellinus, had the guard proclaim 72-year-old Servius Sulpicius Galba as emperor even while Nero lived. After the Senate concurred, Sabinus got Tigellinus to resign and took over as sole prefect.

The two of them had promised the guard a bounty of 7,500 denarii each, an impossibly large sum. Galba, arriving in Rome, made it known that he had no intention of paying it. With that, it became clear that, however much the praetorians might have hoped otherwise, replacing a young emperor with a septuagenarian was not going to bring tranquility to Rome. Galba named as his prefect a long-time follower, Cornelius Laco, whereupon Sabinus attempted a revolt. He claimed the empire as his own, asserting that he was a son of the former emperor Caligula. His effort to persuade the guard, however, was monumentally unsuccessful; when he arrived at the praetorian barracks to make his case, the guards seized and killed him.

Meanwhile, the legions in Germany were becoming displeased with Galba for not paying them the promised bounty. They asked the guard to depose him and find a better man. Galba was also unpopular with the general run of Romans. Tigellinus, the much-hated prefect who had been set aside by Sabinus, had not been executed by Galba as the people wanted, even though the guard, too, had wanted Tigellinus dead. In explanation, Galba said that Tigellinus was a sick man and that he didn't want a reputation for cruelty.

Sensing his increasing unpopularity, Galba decided to name a successor and coadjutor. He selected L. Calpurnius Piso, a fine man but one without much popular support. At the praetorian camp, he proclaimed Piso's new position to an assembly of not very enthusiastic soldiers, whose response turned even more chilly when he failed to announce a donative.

Piso's selection was especially galling to M. Salvius Otho, former governor of Lusitania and a Galba supporter who had himself expected to be named successor. Otho had established a good relationship with the guard. Each time he went to see Galba he gave a gold piece to each praetorian on duty. Now, accompanied by a small detachment of disgruntled praetorians, he gained admission to the castra praetoria and there persuaded the guard as a whole to proclaim him. Needless to say, he promised a very handsome donative. Later in the day he presented himself to the senate and made it appear that he was taking over as emperor reluctantly.

As soon as Otho had been acclaimed by the senate ("confirmed" might be the apter word, for by now the guard clearly exercised the higher power), a detachment was sent to execute Galba. Tacitus gives a vivid if not altogether precise account of the killing. Galba was being carried to the forum on a litter, mobs were in the street, and the guard was controlling key points. The guard seems to have abandoned Galba except for one centurion, Sempronius Densus, who fought off the attackers for some time until he himself was killed. It is unclear who actually killed Galba. The most likely assassin was a soldier of the Legion IV Primigenia, probably one of the men who had been drafted from the Rhineland and brought to Rome by Nero in preparation for the proposed campaign in the Caucasus. At about the same time, on Otho's orders, Piso and the guard prefect Cornelius Laco were killed.

The six months before Otho came to power had been unusually active ones for the guard; the ninety days of his reign (15 January to 15 April 69) were traumatic. Not only was prefect Laco killed by Otho but so also was Tigellinus, Nero's prefect whom Galba had spared. Two new praetorian prefects were then appointed, Plotius Firmus and Licinius Proculis. Some historians say they were selected by the guardsmen themselves. This could be true, for it is known that Plotius Firmus had risen from the ranks and served as commander of the watch. Once installed, the two new prefects were quick to address the guard, century by century, appealing for full support of Otho and promising a donative of five thousand sesterces each.

The importance of the guard at this time and its continued relationship with troops in the field is demonstrated by the mission to Rome of a centurion named Sisenna.

Sisenna was sent from the army in Syria to the praetorian guard in Rome bearing the traditional symbol of mutual hospitality—clasped hands cast in either bronze or silver. In the field, guardsmen and legionnaires generally lived in an atmosphere of trust. In Rome, however, the praetorians were inclined, and probably trained, to be suspicious. Not surprisingly, therefore, when Sisenna arrived at the guard's depot at night to pick up the weapons his command had requisitioned, a number of guards read his action as preparation for an uprising. The guards then invaded the palace where Otho was entertaining at dinner. It was with great difficulty that Otho convinced them that they should go back to their quarters and that his guests had no intention of killing him. The next day Otho went to the camp and made an additional donative of 1,250 drachmas to each man.

A short time after Otho's installation, word came to the praetorians that the legions in lower Germany had decided to name their own emperor and had selected Aulus Vitellius, whom Otho had put in command of the army of lower Germany. Vitellius had previously served well as proconsul of Africa.

Vitellius moved promptly to take over the empire, which meant taking over Rome. In Rome, Otho organized his forces to oppose the legions coming from the north. The army of upper Germany, however, joined with that of lower Germany in the invasion of Italy. Although the legions on the Danube remained loyal to Otho, most of them moved to intervene too late. Narbonese Gaul went over to Vitellius, but a scratch force from

Rome made up of praetorians and auxiliaries put down this local uprising. When Otho sent a mission to Vitellius offering to share the empire, the mission went over to Vitellius, although the praetorians escorting it were allowed to return to Rome in good order.

Finally, Otho took to the field with an army of five praetorian cohorts, elements of four legions from Dalmatia and Pannonia, one newly formed legion, auxiliaries, and a personal body guard of *speculatores*. His force, 25,000 strong, was smaller than that of Vitellius, which was close to 100,000. Despite this, in the first engagement Otho's troops, under command of the praetorian prefect Proculus, gained a sharp success. Otho, however, had held back a large part of his force, including four praetorian cohorts, so when Vitellius's main forces struck, Proculus suffered a severe reverse, and thus ended the first battle of Cremona. Neither Vitellius nor Otho was present.[4]

Shortly before this main engagement, Otho had had a minor victory at Placentia, twenty miles southwest of Cremona. There three cohorts of praetorians, with attachments, defeated a much larger force of Vitellians. This had no more effect on the final outcome than had Otho's earlier success in Narbonese Gaul. After the defeat near Cremona, however, Otho found this small comfort and decided that his cause was hopeless. At Brixellium, where he was then encamped with those forces he had not used, he announced that he planned to kill himself; he wanted no more killing of Roman troops by Roman troops. Proculus and the praetorians tried to dissuade him, to no avail; once Otho was dead, the troops went over to Vitellius. There was no more fighting. Plutarch credits another prefect, Pollio, with getting the praetorians to accept Vitellius, after which the senate perfunctorily gave him the imperial powers.

Suicides have figured several times in this study. It seems appropriate, therefore, to digress briefly and consider the Roman way of death.

Unlike the leaders of other peoples, the Roman ruling classes seem to have taken little interest in a life after death. The Egyptians and others of this time provided elaborate funerals and buried their leaders with all the equipment for a life in the hereafter. The Romans, on the other hand, cremated their dead leaders with pomp and ceremony but with little notion of another life. The Roman gods were gods for the living and might or might not be helpful in life. In fact, sometimes the gods were the creation of the mortal men of the senate, who deified deceased emperors and on occasion de-deified them. Christianity, which took hold among the less successful individuals in the Roman world, had little or no impact on the ruling classes. That there would be a resurrection of the body and eternal life thereafter was an alien and almost inconceivable idea.

The dying emperor Hadrian wrote a poem speculating where his spirit might go after his death. He asks what sort of a dismal place will receive it, a place where the usual jests would be wanting.

> "O blithe little soul, thou, flitting away,
> Guest and comrade of this my clay,
> Whither now goest thou, to what place
> Bare and ghastly and without grace?
> Nor, as thy wont was, joke and play."*

Hadrian sees himself terminated but the spirit surviving, although in a not very pleasant place.

Not uncommonly, Roman leaders resorted to suicide as a way of making an important political statement. Probably the most dramatic example of death for such a purpose was that of centurion Julius Agrestis. A confidant of Vitellius, Agrestis had urged the emperor to take forceful action against the army of Vespasian, which was advancing against Rome. Vitellius procrastinated but finally authorized Agrestis to go north and have a look at the forces serving Vespasian. In the north the centurion was well received, permitted to see all the troops and their condition, and came back to Rome to tell the emperor the true situation. This he did, but Vitellius refused to believe him. Saying he knew of only one way to convince the emperor that he was telling the truth, Agrestis left the room and killed himself.

---

*Translated by A. O'Brien-Moore for the *Augustan History*.

This did convince Vitellius, who then got busy organizing his forces.

The first imperial suicide was that of the thirty-year-old Nero, who had been made emperor at the age of sixteen through the machinations of his mother, Agrippina II, great-granddaughter of the emperor Augustus. Nero was the last emperor of the family of Julius Caesar. After fleeing Rome in the face of an uprising and senatorial condemnation, he killed himself, thereby preventing the kind of undignified maltreatment that was later to be handed out to Vitellius and in 238 to two other emperors, Maximus and Balbinus. Nero gave his death what dignity he could by preceding his suicide with a prayer, largely an aside to Jupiter to the effect that in his death the world was losing a great artist.

Otho was the second emperor known to take his own life. Others were Maximian in 310 and Gordian I in 238. Although the records are not clear, it appears that both Gallus in 251 and Quintillus in 270 also killed themselves.

The case of Otho is a particularly interesting one for he ensured that his initial military defeat by Vitellius would not lead to the shedding of more Roman blood. As mentioned earlier, Otho compared the capabilities of his forces with those of his enemy and resolved not to permit another bloody battle between Romans. Already thousands had died. To forestall further bloodshed, Otho took his own life, arranging it so that his loyal followers would be elsewhere and therefore not liable to charges that they had killed him.

Maximian's suicide followed not a short reign, as did Otho's, but a long and complicated one. In 286 Diocletian made him co-emperor, charged with the care of the western part of the empire. A fine general, Maximian did a good job and retired with Diocletian in 305, although with great reluctance. When Maximian's son, Maxentius, became emperor in Rome, Maximian came out of retirement, first to help his son and then to try to take over the job himself. Failing to get control, he fled to Arles where his son-in-law, Constantine, was emperor. While Constantine was away on the frontier, he organized a revolt, apparently unable to keep his hands off power. The revolt collapsed with the return of Constantine, who then pursued Maximian to Marseilles. There in 310 the old emperor was allowed to commit suicide with some dignity. Constantine, of course, continued on to defeat Maxentius and in due course become head of a unified Roman Empire.

A somewhat less involved suicide was that of Poenius Postumas, camp prefect of XX Valeria Victrix in Britain in 61. In that year Boudicca led the uprising of the Britons that resulted in London's destruction and thousands of casualties for the Romans. The prefect had failed to respond promptly to orders to join the main Roman army, the initial defeat of which could be blamed on the absence of XX Valeria Victrix. His sense of honor and his pride in his profession required Postumas to kill himself. He fell on his sword. This attitude toward failed duty is common in Japanese history but rare in the West.

In Rome itself a considerable number of suicides came about because of the tax laws. During this period the estate of a convicted and executed enemy of the state was forfeited to the state; his heirs received nothing. Conversely, an accused person who committed suicide before conviction could expect his will to be honored, particularly if he left some portion of his estate to the emperor, a not unusual practice.

Gnaeus C. Piso committed suicide in this situation. Then governor of Syria, he was accused of arranging the poisoning of the great general Germanicus. He returned to Rome from Africa convinced that he could clear his name. To his dismay, the emperor Tiberius permitted the case to go to the senate. Knowing that Tiberius had not been overly fond of Germanicus, Piso had hoped that the matter would be settled quietly. When the senate began debate, however, he saw that he probably would be convicted. That evening he retired to his bedroom after supper and killed himself with his sword.

Soldiers and political leaders were not alone in adopting the special attitude toward death discussed here. Men of letters did, too; Anneus Seneca being an excellent example. This prolific writer was for some years the tutor of the young emperor Nero and as long as Nero accepted his guidance Rome had good leadership. Seneca's advice, however, became less and less attractive to Nero and in due course, becoming aware of the emperor's changed attitude, Seneca retired from the court. Accused of participating in the abortive revolt of 65, he was forced to commit suicide, which he did with high drama. Having opened his veins, he continued to dictate the book he was working on as he slowly bled to death. His wife tried to die with him, opening her veins as well. When Seneca was dead, her veins were bound up, apparently against her wishes. She survived.

Seneca's views on religion and suicide are fairly clear in his writings. He wrote a satire on the deification of Claudius which he called "pumpkinification." It expresses his view on the habit of the senate of creating gods and goddesses for political reasons. In another writing he advocates suicide as both a duty and a privilege.

One aspect of the Roman way of death that is not too unlike the Western thinking of today was the general idea of dying with your boots on. When the emperor Vespasian was on the verge of death in 79, he insisted that he be helped by his attendants to stand and walk, saying that an emperor should die on his feet. Half a century later, the praetorian prefect W. Marcius Turbo, who served Hadrian so faithfully, was reproved for working long, killing hours. His response was the same, that prefects should die on their feet.

Unlike the pomposity with which leaders in the Western world have made deathbed remarks, the Romans could and did mix a bit of wit with their dying. Both Dio and Suetonius reported Vespasian's poking a bit of fun at the senate's habit of deifying deceased emperors. As death approached, he said, probably with a wry smile, that he must now be turning into a god. When he was brought word of an ill omen—a comet streaking across the sky —, he remarked that it was obviously an omen for the King of Parthia, who had long hair like the tail of a comet; it could not be for himself, for he was bald. One can think of no departing leader in our own time who has greeted death with such disrespect.

In summary, the special view of death described here combines an acceptance of suicide with little or no belief in life after death but a strong belief in the fitness of things. The concept may be said to have three aspects, the first of which was suicide for the good of the state, as in the cases of Otho and Postumas. The second was suicide for the good of the family, as exemplified by Piso and Seneca. The third was having one's death conform with certain ideal standards, as in the cases of Turbo and Vespasian.

Returning now to the days following Otho's death, we find the Vitellian commanders distributing the praetorian cohorts to half a dozen places in northern Italy, with two cohorts at Turin. One historian[5] speculates that these two were to act as an imperial escort for Vitellius when he entered Italy from Gaul. In any event, they were probably used as a nucleus for a reorganized guard.

One of the first acts of Vitellius was to dismiss most of the praetorians, giving them honorable discharges and their previously earned financial rights. He then reconstituted the guard cohorts with men from the German legions, increasing the number of cohorts to sixteen.

Until this time the guard had been essentially Italian in background, so the new German praetorians were resented by the populace of Rome. Publius Sabinus and Julius Priscus were named praetorian prefects. Sabinus had been the prefect of an auxiliary cohort, presumably in Germany. Priscus was a centurion. By this reorganization, Vitellius had created an eight-thousand-man force in Rome itself that was personally loyal to him. In fighting power it was equal to two legions.

The need for such a loyal force soon became apparent, for the long shadow of Titus Flavius Vespasian fell over Italy. Vespasian was at Caesarea, on the Mediterranean coast of Palestine, conducting the war against the Jews when word reached him of Vitellius's seizure of power. A great general and a natural leader of men, Vespasian was proclaimed emperor 1 July 69 by the legions in Palestine, and shortly thereafter by those in Syria and Egypt. The legions on the Danube, in Moesia, and in Pannonia soon followed suit. Vespasian moved his headquarters to Alexandria to ensure control of the grain supply that was shipped from there to Rome, and Mucianus, one of his most trusted generals, was designated to lead the advance on Rome.

Back in the capital, Vitellius showed little concern. He did, however, dismiss and jail Sabinus, one of his newly appointed praetorian prefects, because of Sabinus's friendship with one of Vitellius's generals, Caeacena, who had gone over to the side of Vespasian. In his place he appointed Alfenus Varus, who was to play an important part in the defense of Rome.

As the legions of Vespasian moved up through the Danube area for the invasion of Italy, Vitellius organized his legions from Gaul and Germany for defense, augmenting them with elements from the three legions in Britain. While the forthcoming battle was taking shape, the dismissed praetorians were not forgotten by Vespasian's agents. In Narbonese Gaul they were recruited by Valerius Paulinus and formed again into cohorts of the guard. Paulinus had been a tribune of the guard, and from all over northern Italy the guardsmen flocked to his command, hoping for revenge against those soldiers from the Germanic legions who were now called praetorians in Rome.

The main engagement between the two armies took place near Cremona, not far from the site of Vitellius's victory over Otho earlier in the year. The forces in this second battle of Cremona were fairly evenly balanced, with six legions and the elements from Britain on the Vitellian side and five legions and the reconstituted praetorians on the Flavian side. Both armies had the usual auxiliaries attached. The engagement was fiercely fought through the night of 24 October and the following day. As in the first battle of Cremona, neither claimant to the empire was present. The praetorian cohorts held the right of the Flavian line with III Gallica on their left and auxiliary cavalry on the flank. This put them face to face with I Germanicus. When the Vitellians drove back Vespasian's VII Gemina, the praetorians were slipped to the left where they restored the situation. Some measure of the quality of these troops is that they successfully executed the most difficult of all military maneuvers, a lateral movement at night while engaged with the enemy. But in their new position they found themselves in trouble, for the enemy poured on them the fire of concentrated catapults. In the darkness, two praetorians, disguising themselves with the

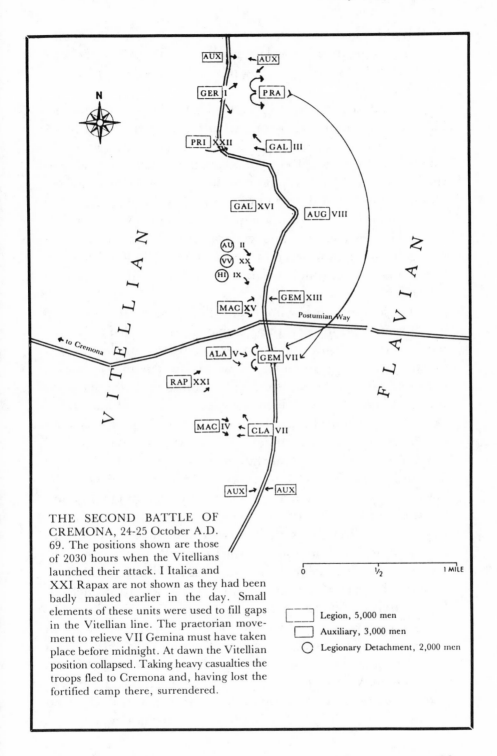

THE SECOND BATTLE OF
CREMONA, 24-25 October A.D.
69. The positions shown are those
of 2030 hours when the Vitellians
launched their attack. I Italica and
XXI Rapax are not shown as they had been
badly mauled earlier in the day. Small
elements of these units were used to fill gaps
in the Vitellian line. The praetorian movement to relieve VII Gemina must have taken
place before midnight. At dawn the Vitellian
position collapsed. Taking heavy casualties the
troops fled to Cremona and, having lost the
fortified camp there, surrendered.

☐ Legion, 5,000 men
☐ Auxiliary, 3,000 men
◯ Legionary Detachment, 2,000 men

shields of enemy casualties, worked themselves into the enemy line and cut the ropes of the largest catapult. They were of course recognized and killed, but they probably saved the praetorian position.

As said earlier, Tacitus had no love for the praetorians and, like most of the historians of antiquity, he shamelessly made up speeches for attribution to leaders. It is odd, however, to find him venting his spleen writing about this battle. He reports that Antonius Primus, commander of Vespasian's forces, addressed the reconstituted praetorian cohorts, telling them that they should be ashamed of themselves. Tacitus would have us believe that a commanding general in the midst of a night engagement made a speech to several thousand soldiers fighting desperately to hold their position. In this case Tacitus outdid himself.

There are some who claim that it was the vengeful praetorians who insured the Flavian victory. Others give the palm to III Gallica, Vespasian's own. It was this legion that greeted the rising sun on the twenty-fifth with the shouts customary in Syria at sunrise, and so confused their opponents that they thought III Gallica was being reinforced and therefore retreated. On the twenty-fifth the Vitellians fell back on Cremona and later surrendered. They were marched out in ignominy between lines of the victorious Flavians.

In Rome, Vitellius found it most difficult to believe in the defeat of his forces in the north, but finally he began to organize for the defense of Rome. Under the command of his two praetorian prefects, he sent fourteen cohorts of his guard with orders to hold the line of the Apennines. With them he sent the newly formed legion, II Adiutrix, and some auxiliary cavalry. The remaining two cohorts of the guard he held in Rome itself under command of his brother, Lucius.

All eyes were now fixed on the north, where the Flavian forces were advancing slowly toward Rome and Vitellius's troops were concentrating at Narnia under the prefects Julius Priscus and Alfenus Varus. The Flavians halted at Fanum Fortunae, and negotiations were carried out over a considerable period of time. Gradually, the Vitellians either surrendered or came over to the Flavian side, until only the guard remained in a form to resist.

Unexpectedly, to the south of Rome at Terracina, the Vitellian leader Julianus went over to the Flavian side. Vitellius then sent from Narnia six of the fourteen guard cohorts to put down the uprising in the Campania. In command he placed Lucius, who in due course arrived and recaptured Terracina and then sent a message to Vitellius asking for further orders. By this time, though, it was too late for Lucius to intervene in Rome, for the army at Narnia had collapsed. After Rome's fall, Lucius surrendered. His cohorts were disarmed and marched to imprisonment. He was taken to Rome and executed.

Meanwhile, at Narnia the departure of Priscus and Varus for Rome appears to have been a signal for the formal surrender that soon followed. On 18 December Vitellius learned of the general surrender at Narnia and tried to abdicate. He was not permitted to do this by his more ardent followers, and it became clear that Rome was to be a battleground. To prevent this, Vespasian's brother, Flavius Sabinus, who, above politics, had faithfully performed the duties of city prefect, tried to confine the troops to barracks. They refused to obey. He then occupied the Capitoline Hill with a mixed force and had with him Domitian, the young son of Vespasian and a future emperor. The Vitellian praetorians assaulted the hill on 19 December, killed most of those who were there, and burned to the ground the temple of Jupiter. Domitian was one of the few to escape. Sabinus was taken to Vitellius, who tried unsuccessfully to protect him from the troops. Sabinus was killed.

On 20 December, after heavy street fighting, Rome was captured by the Flavian forces under command of Licinius Mucianus, Vespasians's army commander. The Flavian forces crossed the Tiber at the Milvian Bridge, sweeping aside Vitellian resistance. Flavian cavalry was used to ford the Tiber and clear the bridge area, whereupon the army divided into three columns. One moving southward followed the Via Flaminia, the second advanced along the left bank of the Tiber, and the third, containing the Flavian praetorians, moved southeastward toward the castra praetoria. This third column met heavy resistance approaching the castra and once there faced a strong defense by the Vitellian praetorians. The Vitellians fought desperately to hold the fort; the praetorians of Vespasian fought with wild determination to get back what they considered their barracks. It was a prolonged fight between highly skilled soldiers. The walls were assaulted. Catapults were used. A heavy fire of spears and stones was poured on the attackers, and at least one sally in force was made by the Vitellians. Finally, the fortress gate was torn from its hinges and the Flavians were able to fight their way into the camp. There the fighting continued until the Vitellian praetorians were virtually exterminated by their Flavian predecessors.

Shortly thereafter, Mucianus and Domitian arrived in Rome. Domitian made a speech to the guard, giving each of them a hundred sesterces. There remained, however, the problem of what to do with the imprisoned Vitellian praetorians who had been marched back from Terracina. Passions by now having subsided, they were assembled under guard of the Flavian praetorians and were either retired, reassigned to the legions from which they had been drawn, or in some cases actually assigned to the Flavian praetorian cohorts. Julius Priscus, one of the two Vitellian praetorian prefects, committed suicide; the other, Alfenus Varus, seems to have survived.

The new prefect appointed by Mucianus was Arrius Varus, a vigorous officer who had served under Corbulo in Armenia, where he became a senior centurion. He had participated in the occupation of Aquileia and in the second battle of Cremona. He was also a friend of Domitian. With this background, he turned out to be too strong a personality for Mucianus, who relieved him as prefect and controller of the corn supply. In his place he put Arrecinus Clemens, a relative of Vespasian and also a friend of Domitian. Clemens's father had been praetorian prefect under Caligula. He was of senatorial rank, which made his appointment unusual; normally the prefects were drawn from the equestrian class.

Troubles broke out in the north with the revolt of Civilis, and Mucianus and Domitian set out to put things right. Presumably, several cohorts of the guard accompanied Domitian since he was the emperors's son, but Mucianus persuaded Domitian to stay at Lyon rather than continuing north to complete the campaign, so presumably the guardsmen saw little or no action.

Vespasian finally arrived in Rome during the summer. Believing that a praetorian guard of sixteen cohorts was too large and too expensive, he reduced it to nine, apparently more through attrition than by wholesale dismissal or forced retirement. In due course he made his son Titus sole praetorian prefect. Titus, who had successfully completed the war against the Jews, served in fact as virtual co-emperor, a rare case of father and son working in complete harmony.

The castra must have observed with interest Vespasian's ceremonial closing of the doors to the temple of Janus A.D. 70. For centuries, the closing of the doors of this small temple on the north side of the Roman forum was the signal that throughout the Roman world there was peace. Janus was the god of beginnings, of departures, of setting forth, and of the doorway of the home. When his temple doors were opened, it meant that the emperor was starting off to the wars, probably taking much of the guard with him.

In 29 B.C. Augustus had closed these doors to show Rome that he had brought peace to the empire. It was but the third time that the doors had been closed. He again had them closed in 25 B.C., and A.D. 66 Nero similarly proclaimed peace.*

Titus Flavius Sabinus Vespasianus, appointed praetorian prefect A.D. 69 by his father, Vespasian. After ten years as prefect he succeeded his father as emperor but died two years later.

---

*The last time a door ceremony took place was not to close but to open them; this was in 242 on the occasion of Gordian III's departure from Rome, together with most of his praetorians, for the great expedition against the Persians.

When Vespasian died in 79, Titus became emperor, although he had something less than the wholehearted support of his brother Domitian. On the contrary, there is some evidence that Domitian participated in a number of unsuccessful plots against Titus, who naively continued to seek his cooperation. Few records of this period cite the guard, and the names of Titus's prefects do not come to hand.

Titus died in 81. When he was on his deathbed, Domitian went to the castra praetoria and had himself proclaimed emperor. He made a donative equal to that which Titus had given at his elevation.

Domitian's reign was marked by the use of the guard cohorts on the frontiers, particularly in Dacia. Although Domitian took part in the Dacian campaign, he kept himself well away from combat. Cornelius Fuscus, a prefect of the guard, was killed in this campaign. Domitian had also gone to the German frontier, presumably with much of the guard, but he himself saw no action there.

The increasing influence of the praetorians is shown in the appointment of two prefects of Egypt as praetorian prefects, a reversal of precedent. Earlier, praetorian prefect Lucius Julius Ursus had been prefect of Egypt and went on to be consul in 83. His successor, appointed in 84, was Lucius Laberius Maximus, then prefect of Egypt. A portion of the appointment letter to Maximus survives.[6]

As for the guard itself, Domitian increased the number of cohorts from nine to ten to ensure security in Rome while most of the guard was away with him. He also increased praetorian base pay from 750 denarii to a thousand.

At this time there seems to have been a rather rapid turnover of praetorian prefects. By the year 96 the prefects were Norbanus and Petronius Secundus, both of whom had a keen dislike for the emperor. Despite the fact that most of the guard was still loyal to Domitian, these two prefects participated in a successful plot to do away with him. Casperius Aelianus, who had served as prefect for Domitian, apparently was not involved. On 18 September 96, the conspirators murdered Domitian when he had retired in the afternoon for a rest after holding court.

He was not killed, however, until his murderers had selected a successor, Marcus Cocceius Nerva.

Word of the murder of the last of the Flavians was not well received by the praetorians. For some time they morosely held their peace. Finally, under the leadership of Nerva's newly reappointed prefect, Casperius Aelianus, they revolted and seized the palace. They then demanded that Nerva execute those responsible for Domitian's murder. Nerva at first resisted their demands, offering his own throat to their weapons, but in the end he was prevailed upon to hand over former prefect Petronius Secundus and other conspirators, who were promptly killed. Nerva was then forced to publicly thank the praetorians for killing Petronius.

The eighteen months following the ascension of Nerva were bad ones for praetorian prefects. Norbanus, who had been replaced by Aelianus, disappears from history. Nerva died after a rule of only sixteen months. Trajan, who succeeded him in 98, immediately summoned Aelianus and others who had participated in the revolt, asking them to meet him in Cologne as if he had an important mission for them. When they arrived he put them out of the way.

The nineteen and a half years of Trajan's rule were years of great military victories. Unfortunately, history does not record which legions he used at which time or the number of praetorian cohorts that accompanied him and the number that remained in Rome. History does record, however, much greater use of his praetorian prefects and centurions in diplomatic missions. This was a trend that would continue during the reigns of future emperors, when not only army command and diplomacy fell to the lot of the praetorian prefects but also the codification of law and administration of the courts.

Trajan wisely made a handsome donative to the praetorians when he came to power. It may be assured that a number of the cohorts were with him in the two Dacian campaigns with which his rule started. We know that the prefect Claudius Livianus was with him, for Livianus was sent forward by Trajan to negotiate with the Dacian king, Decebalus. The latter, however, avoided the meeting. The two campaigns ended with a victory for Trajan and death for Decebalus. Gratifyingly, sometime during these battles the Romans recaptured the standards that had been lost when the Dacians had defeated and killed Domitian's prefect, Cornelius Fuscus. Apparently, Roman armies were most successful when the emperor himself took the field, particularly when he was a man of such military prowess as Trajan.

Several historians tell a story that illustrates an interesting aspect of Trajan's character. When Trajan decided to make Saburanus prefect of the praetorians, he presented Saburanus with the sword of office, drew it from the scabbard, and told him that if, as emperor, he ruled well Saburanus was to use the sword for him; but, if he ruled badly, Saburanus was to use it against him.

Trajan spent the last years of his life campaigning in the East. There he not only captured the Persian capital of Ctesiphon but swept down the Tigris and Euphrates to the Persian Gulf, passing through Babylon on the way. He would have liked to have gone on, as Alexander did, into India, but his health and the exhaustion of his troops would not permit. It was during this campaign in 116 that praetorians were again used as envoys. The centurion Sentius, presumably a praetorian, was sent to negotiate with Mebarsapes, king of Adiabene, that part of Assyria that included Ninevah. Unwisely, the king imprisoned Sentius at a strong post called Adenystrae. As the Romans approached, Sentius and other prisoners succeeded in breaking their bonds. Under Sentius's leadership they effectively engaged the garrison, killed its commander, and opened the gates to advancing Roman forces.

Trajan was not to see Rome again, for in 117, after his return to his headquarters, he had what appears to have been a stroke and died. Publius Aelius Hadrian, his cousin and ward, assumed command in Syria and was acknowledged as emperor. There is some question as to whether Trajan had in reality designated him his successor, but it would have been a wise step. In any event, Rome believed the report and accepted Hadrian as the new ruler.

Two

The Danube
and Raphanaea

At the time Hadrian came to power the praetorian prefects were Aneilius Attianus and C. Sulpicius Similis. With Trajan, Attianus had been co-guardian of Hadrian when Hadrian was a youth, and he was a devoted but over-enthusiastic supporter, taking it on himself to arrange the deaths of a number of individuals who he thought were plotting against his emperor. Displeased, Hadrian decided to get rid of him. On his return to Rome, some eleven months after becoming emperor, Hadrian asked Attianus to resign, at the same time offering him senatorial rank, which he said was the greatest gift in the emperor's power to make. The other prefect, C. Sulpicius Similis, was an old soldier who had risen from the ranks, shown great distinction, and been prefect of Egypt before becoming praetorian prefect. He now wanted to resign because of his age, which Hadrian reluctantly permitted him to do.

To replace the two, Hadrian chose Marcius Turbo, a loyal follower who had had a distinguished military career under Trajan. Given to working long hours, Marcius was once asked by Hadrian why he did not take some rest. His reply was a quote from Vespasian, slightly altered: a prefect should die on his feet.

In his choice for the second praetorian prefect, the poet Septicius Clarus, Hadrian was not so fortunate. Clarus was a friend of the younger Pliny and of the historian Suetonius, who held the court office of imperial secretary. Clarus and Suetonius were both dismissed from their posts for not showing proper respect for the empress. Clarus was replaced by Gavius Maximus, who was to serve as prefect for twenty years.

The historians tell many stories about Hadrian, one of which points to his pride in the guard. When a youth petitioned him to be allowed to join the praetorians, Hadrian asked the boy how tall he was. The boy replied that he was five feet, six inches. Hadrian told the youth that he was to serve two terms in the city guard and then, when he was six feet tall, he could transfer to the praetorians.

Hadrian made the praetorians the example, par excellence, for the army as a whole. He insisted on the highest level of training and was known to use some of the guard's centurions as training officers with the legions or auxiliary forces.

His several generous donatives must have been most welcome at the castra praetoria, for those who followed the emperor had a busy life far from home. Hadrian traveled far and long, starting in 121 on an empire tour that lasted five years and included Britain, Provence, Spain, North Africa, Greece, and Turkey. He came back to Rome by way of Sicily where, presumably with some reluctant praetorians, he climbed Mount Etna. After a year in Rome, he was off again to Carthage, Athens, Antioch, Petra, Palestine, and Alexandria. He returned to Rome in 134 and died four years later.

Possibly the saddest duty that the two prefects, Marcus Turbo and Gavius Maximus, had to perform was that of preventing the emperor's suicide. Very ill and tired of life, after naming Antoninus Pius his successor, Hadrian tried to kill himself. His dagger was taken from him, however, and the two prefects and Antoninus implored him to live as long as possible. He moved to his palace at Baia not far from Naples and died there in the presence of Antoninus on 10 July 138.

The praetorians had little history during the twenty-three-year rule of Antoninus, who stayed in Rome and let his generals conduct such minor campaigns as took place on the frontiers. The guardsmen received several handsome donatives and seem to have been pleased with a relatively uneventful period. Neither Antoninus Pius nor his successor received the imperial office as a result of murder or revolt. Wisely, the emperor kept Turbo and Maximus in office. Maximus, who first served with Turbo and later, in 143, as sole prefect, was ideal for the job. An Italian by birth, he had served as *procurator* both in Mauretania and in Asia before being appointed prefect about 130. He was undoubtedly Antoninus's chief adviser on military matters and foreign relations. Having been granted consular insignia, he retired, probably before 156. He was replaced as praetorian prefect by Tatius Maximus, then prefect of the watch. Tatius also served as sole prefect, but was replaced by two men. The emperor thus returned to the Augustan concept of the joint command, naming as prefects Furius Victorinus and Cornelius Repentinus. The latter created a whisper of scandal when rumor had it that his appointment resulted from the intervention of Galeria Lysistrata, the emperor's beautiful concubine. Among the outstanding legal experts that the emperor employed was Salvius Julianus, who was to be appointed a praetorian prefect himself by Commodus about 190.

Aged seventy-five, Antoninus died in March of 161 at Lorium in the presence of his two prefects and Marcus Aurelius, his son-in-law and designated heir.

Castra praetoria was visited almost at once by the new emperor, Marcus Aurelius, who had named as co-emperor Lucius Verus, the other adopted son of Antoninus Pius. Verus, speaking for both of them, promised 20,000 sesterces for each soldier and proportionately more for each officer.

When trouble broke out in the East, Verus went there to put things in order, undoubtedly accompanied by an element of the guard. Fighting also broke out on the Danube front. The praetorian prefect, Furius Victorinus, who had served Antoninus Pius so well, died there either in combat or from a plague that swept over the army. Verus, who had proved to be something of a lightweight, died in January 168. Thereafter, Marcus Aurelius ruled alone.

Although much admired as a philosopher, Marcus Aurelius spent most of his time in the field fighting Rome's enemies. With him the praetorians traveled far and often—to the East, to Germany, and to the Danube front. Marcus made his headquarters for some years at Vienna and died there on 17 March 180. Back in Rome were two praetorian prefects, Bassaeus Rufus and Macrinius Vindex. They were in charge of administration and undoubtedly commanded the troops remaining in the castra. In 169 Vindex was sent north to engage the invading Germans and died in combat there. With Marcus on the Danube front was another praetorian prefect, Tarrutienus Paternus, who outlived the emperor and served his son and successor, Commodus.

With the accession of Commodus, the castra found itself for the second time with a teenage emperor. The results were even more unpleasant than those that followed Nero's coming to power. Nero was sixteen when he began his rule, Commodus eighteen. Nero ruled for thirteen years and Commodus twelve. Both were dissolute and, if the *Augustan History* is to be believed, Commodus did, in fact, order the burning of Rome, which was prevented only by the intervention of the praetorian prefect, Aemilius Laetus.

Marcus Aurelius had set up an advisory council that was supposed to guide the first steps of his young son, and the praetorian prefect Tarrutienus Paternus was outstanding among the advisers. The young emperor, however, did not take readily to the advice proffered him, since it would have him stay on the Danube front and complete the work begun by his father. Against even the advice of his close friend, praetorian prefect Tigidius Perennis, Commodus insisted on returning to Rome, where life was much more entertaining. On his arrival, he made grateful acknowledgment to the praetorians, accompanied by a handsome donative, and following Claudius's example, put the praetorians on his coinage, one of the few emperors to do so. He pursued a publicly hedonistic life, marked by much banqueting, sexual episodes with both women and boys, and patronage of theatricals and circus performances not unlike those of Nero.

Not surprisingly, the disapproving Paternus became very unpopular with Commodus. On his return to Rome, the emperor had celebrated a triumph, and in his chariot riding behind him was Saoterus, his homosexual lover whom he kissed on occasion during the triumph. Paternus was not pleased. He arranged to have Saoterus led from the court with great respect but had him killed once removed from the palace grounds. Soon thereafter, in 182, Paternus was accused of conspiring to kill the emperor and was executed.

With Paternus gone, Perennis became sole prefect and virtually ran the empire, Commodus having little time for his imperial duties. Despite the fact that Perennis did a good job, or maybe just because he did, he inspired the envy and enmity of Marcus Aurelian Cleander, a former slave and tutor of Commodus, who had risen to court chamberlain. Cleander is credited with arranging Perennis's downfall, achieved when some 1,500 troops from Britain approached Rome. Met outside the city by the emperor, who inquired as to their reason for being there, the troops claimed that they came to warn the emperor against Perennis. Commodus then believed that his praetorian prefect was in fact conspiring against him. He turned Perennis over to the troops from Britain, who killed him on the spot.

The prefect who succeeded Perennis was P. Atilius Aebutianus. Aebutianus also inspired the dislike of Cleander, who arranged the prefect's death in 187. This time Cleander took the job himself. He lasted, however, only three years at most. He was very unpopular with the citizenry of Rome. When, to protest a grain shortage, the people rioted, Cleander ordered the praetorian cavalry to run them down and trample them. Many citizens and praetorians were killed. Commodus's sister, Fadilla, told the emperor that Cleander was aiming to eliminate him and become emperor himself. Cleander was then sent for by Commodus, who had him killed immediately. His two sons were also put to death.

Following Cleander as joint praetorian prefects were Regillus and L. Julius Vehilius Grafus Julianus, both of whom were later killed by Commodus. According to the *Augustan History,* Julianus was pushed into a swimming pool and drowned.

There were several minor co-prefects, including T. Longeus Rufus, former prefect of Egypt, and Motilenus, who was supposed to have been put to death by being fed poisoned figs. Setting something of a record was Pescennius Niger, who lasted just six hours.

In 191, Quintus Aemilius Laetus was made prefect. He proved to be strong enough to outlast both Commodus and his successor. He was saved from execution by the discovery of a tablet on which Commodus had listed the people next to be killed. The list included not only Laetus but also Marcia, the emperor's concubine, into whose hands the list had fallen. She got hold of Laetus and together they disposed of Commodus. She first poisoned him, and then his trainer strangled him to death.[1]

It is a tribute to the organizational efficiency of the Roman state that an emperor such as Commodus did so little harm to the empire's position in the world. Under direction of the senior praetorian prefects, the commanders in the field successfully protected the frontiers. In addition, the governors of the provinces maintained, in general, an orderly existence. There were serious outbreaks in Britain and in other parts of the empire, but the local commanders and the governors handled them with marked effectiveness. It appears that the empire could occasionally afford a Commodus.

For the castra praetoria, the year 193 was a disaster. In the closing days of 192, Commodus, whom the guardsmen regarded highly, was murdered by their own prefect. Pertinax was brought to the castra by Prefect Laetus to be proclaimed emperor, which the praetorians did reluctantly under pressure from a mob of Roman citizens. The senate proclaimed Pertinax with more enthusiasm, for he was a man of distinguished ancestry. Sixty-six years old, he had served as city prefect, had had a fine military record in Germany and the East, and was one of the few remaining men who had been chosen by Marcus Aurelius as advisers to his son. Marcus had publicly stated that he would have made Pertinax praetorian prefect had he not been a senator and thus ineligible.

Within a day of Pertinax's coming to power the guard was virtually in revolt. The emperor had promised a donative of twelve thousand sesterces, but this was cut in half after he had been proclaimed. He first gave as password to the guard, "let us be soldiers," implying that the men of the guard were not. This was taken as a mortal insult. On 3 January, the praetorians tried to install another emperor, a senator named Triarius Maternus Lascivius. The senator refused the honor, reported to Pertinax, and fled the city. Pertinax then paid over to the praetorians the donative that had been promised earlier by Commodus. He tightened the discipline of the praetorians, and a considerable number of soldiers of the guard were executed. These executions enraged some of the guard because they were based solely on the testimony of one slave.

Other military elements in Rome also appear to have been disaffected. It is difficult to interpret from the obviously anti-praetorian histories just exactly what happened on March 28th. Certainly Pertinax was murdered by a group of maybe two hundred soldiers after he had tried to talk them out of it. Most authors state that these soldiers were praetorians, but there is evidence that the killers were *equites singlares* from the north who had a special loyalty to the murdered Commodus; the name of the leader is given by one source as Tausins, from northern Gaul. Why Pertinax did not use the cohort of the guard on duty that day to disperse the assailants is a matter for speculation.

There now being no emperor, the praetorians withdrew into the castra to await developments. Two candidates for the purple presented themselves at the castra: Didius Julianus and Ti. Flavius Sulpicianus. Both made speeches to the praetorians telling of their qualifications and intentions if proclaimed. Julianus, who had the backing of two praetorian tribunes, Publius Florianus and Vectius Aper, announced that he would make a donative of 25,000 sesterces per soldier. He was eventually chosen over Sulpicianus, city prefect and father-in-law of Pertinax, whose proposed donative did not equal that of Julianus.

Historians heap scorn on the castra for selecting an emperor solely because he was the candidate offering the most money. In fact, they chose an excellent man; Didius Julianus had been a protege of Marcus Aurelius and had been brought up in the home of that emperor's mother. He had served as praetor on the commendation of Marcus, commanded legion XXII Primigenia in Germany, and had been governor of Belgica, Dalmatia, and, later, lower Germany. He was consul with Pertinax.

Taking a rather dim view of prefects who assassinated their emperors, Julianus had both Laetus and the concubine Marcia executed. To take the place of Laetus, he appointed two praetorian prefects recommended by the castra, Tullius Crispinus and T. Flavius Genialis; neither was to serve for long.

The immediate problem for Julianus was survival. In Syria, a revolt by Pescennius Niger, with the support of the legions there, proposed to put Niger in the palace. This may be the same Niger who was very briefly praetorian prefect under Commodus. In Pannonia, the legions on the Danube front put forward their commander, Septimus Severus, as emperor. The legions in Gaul and Germany also supported Severus.

The Niger uprising was less threatening than that of Severus. The latter organized quickly and moved with picked legions on Rome. So many military leaders went over to Severus that Julianus was left with little more than the praetorians to protect Rome. The emperor sent off prefect Tullius Crispinus to Ravenna, where he was supposed to organize the fleet to support the emperor. Crispinus was met, however, by forces friendly to Severus and driven back. The situation having deteriorated further, Julianus had the senate name him and Severus co-emperors. He then dispatched Crispinus to meet Severus and negotiate an arrangement. When Crispinus met the advance guard of Severus's troops, he was promptly put to death. The fate of the other prefect, Flavius Genialis, is not known.

About this time, Julianus made a rather statesman-like move. Severus had informed a Veturius Macrinus that Macrinus would be praetorian prefect when Severus reached Rome. Julianus learned of this appointment and himself appointed Macrinus praetorian prefect, thus providing a transitional commander.

At the castra praetoria, preparations were going forward in a rather desultory manner for the defense of Rome. The tribunes and leading centurions received letters from Severus promising them much if they would obey his instructions. Orders were then issued openly to the troops to come out from Rome in ceremonial dress, not armored, to welcome the new emperor. By this time, the senate had given up on Julianus and ordered his execution, which took place on 1 June 193.

As ordered, the guard marched out of Rome to welcome Severus. They were, however, surrounded by Severus's troops and read a lecture by the new emperor on the subject of their evil doings. He then dismissed them all from the service. This episode is described in loving detail by several historians but does not ring true. If the praetorian prefect, the tribunes, and leading centurions were all informed in advance, one can assume that those who turned out for dismissal by Severus were but a portion of the guard. It is more than possible that the centurions unloaded all the misfits in this exercise and retained their best men. Those who were dismissed and were good soldiers undoubtedly found immediate employment in the depleted legions that had been brought to Rome by Severus. The emperor filled the ranks of the praetorians with men from these legions, thus creating a further demand for legion replacements.

Severus not only filled the guard with his own men but doubled its size. Each of the ten cohorts had its strength raised from 500 to 1,000. With the city troops he went even farther, increasing the size of the four cohorts from 500 to 1,500. The reorganized praetorian guard shared in the donatives made after the emperor's establishment in Rome. What is not clear is the part that this guard was to play in Severus's wars in Syria, Persia, and Gaul. In his final campaign in Britain, Severus took with him a substantial portion of the guard. The troops were under the command of Aemilius Papinianus, appointed praetorian prefect in 205. Shortly after Severus's death in 211 at York, Papinianus was executed in Rome by Caracalla.

Severus had a great deal of experience with praetorian prefects. In Sicily, before he became emperor, he had been accused of treason and tried by the prefects of the guard and found not guilty. On becoming emperor, Severus retained Veturius Macrinus for a time. He also retained another of Julianus's appointees, T. Flavius Genialis, whom he kept in office until 200. Among his prefects were A. Maecius Laetus and Domitius Ulpianus, both distinguished jurists. Laetus served from 205 until possibly 212. One very ambitious prefect, Gaius Fulvius Plautianus, was prefect of both the watch and the praetorians. Plautianus arranged, much to the displeasure of Severus, the marriage of his daughter to Caracalla.

Some historians repeat a tale that Plautianus had 100 boys emasculated and gave them as a wedding present to his daughter. The story is much too pat to be given credence.[2] In 205, he was accused of conspiring to kill both his son-in-law, Caracalla, and the emperor Severus with the intention of taking over the empire himself. He was executed with dispatch.

Two other prefects who served Severus were A. Amilius Saturninus (who, it appears, was killed by Plautianus about 200) and Valerius Patrinus, who was executed when Caracalla became emperor.

During the period that Caracalla was emperor, 211-217, the praetorians were more than busy. The cohorts that had been in Britain returned with the co-emperors Geta and Caracalla. Geta, Caracalla's brother, was murdered in the palace by Caracalla, who then rushed to the castra praetoria where, after a rambling speech, he had himself acclaimed sole emperor. He made then and there a convincing donative of 10,000 sesterces and announced a 50 percent pay raise. Three years later, he was to make an even larger gift of 25,000 per man to those who had accompanied him in the field.

Caracalla spent the first night of his sole rule within the castra, somewhat unsure of his position. Geta had been the more popular of the two brothers. Caracalla was, however, able to get the senate and the closest legion to Rome, II Parthica at Albano, to endorse him. This required personal visits to both, after which Caracalla entered the palace escorted by prefect Papinianus whom, with the other prefect inherited from his father, he was about to execute. To take their places, he appointed as praetorian prefects Marcius Rustius Rufinus and Marcus Opellinus Macrinus. Later, possibly to replace Rufinus, he appointed M. Oclatinus Adventis, an old soldier who had once been a *speculatore* and later a *procurator* in Britain. Macrinus, a native of Morocco, was to become emperor himself, one of four praetorian prefects to do so.

Caracalla was not liked in Rome and spent most of his time in the field with the troops. In Rome he was often jeered; on one occasion, he had the praetorians kill a number of people at a horse race because he felt that he had been insulted.[3]

In the field, Caracalla apparently conducted himself as a good leader, doing everything that he asked his men to do, even to carrying legion standards and marching rather than riding.[4] With his praetorian escort, he went first to the Danube front in 213 and then on to Gaul, Thrace, Armenia, and Alexandria.[5] He then used the praetorians in an initially successful campaign against Parthia, permitting him to overrun Mesopotamia. He made his base at Antioch.

It was near Carrhae in Mesopotamia that Caracalla met his fate. He had spent much time teasing and harassing his praetorian prefect, Macrinus, a man of marked legal abilities. Caracalla had also treated badly, at least in their eyes, some members of the guard. Angered, Macrinus devised a plan for Caracalla's assassination in which there were to be several other participants, including the commanding officer of II Parthica and several members of the guard. The actual killing was done by Julius Martialis, a former soldier. Escorted by cavalry, Caracalla was on the way from Carrhae to the nearby temple of Sin, on or about 8 April 217. When the column stopped for the emperor to relieve himself, he was stabbed to death by Martialis, who was then killed by the emperor's German personal guards. Macrinus, who was included in the escort, expressed great sorrow but then arranged in short order to have himself proclaimed emperor by the army in Syria. A forthcoming major engagement with the Parthians required that a commander take the field, and Macrinus was the obvious choice. The senate in Rome, where Caracalla had never been popular, accepted and confirmed the act of the army in selecting the new emperor. The ensuing battle with the Parthians, in which the praetorians played an important part, came to an indecisive end after three days, when the Parthian commander learned that his real enemy, Caracalla, was dead. Macrinus was then able to negotiate a temporary peace.

The praetorians promptly received from the new emperor a larger-than-usual donative. The prefect M. Oclatinus Adventis was dispatched to Rome with the ashes of Caracalla and instructions to arrange and oversee an appropriate imperial funeral.

During the fifteen months that Macrinus was to be emperor, Adventis handled the Rome end of the job, while the other prefect, Ulpius Julianus, commanded the cohorts in Syria. Macrinus was never to see Rome as emperor; he remained during the entire time in Syria, attempting to put that house in order. The cohorts were undoubtedly stationed in or near Antioch, where Macrinus established his headquarters.

While Macrinus was organizing the eastern part of the empire, an unexpected revolt took place in Antioch. It was organized by Julia Maesa, sister-in-law of the late emperor Severus and aunt of Caracalla, who had spent many influential years in the court in Rome; her eldest daughter, Julia Soemias Bassiana, widow of a Syrian who became a senator in Rome; and Bassiana's youngest daughter, Mamaea Julia Avita, whose Syrian husband had been influential in Caracalla's court. All three had been ordered out of Rome by the emperor Macrinus. On returning to Antioch, the family's home city, they employed their great wealth and diplomatic guile to subvert elements of Macrinus's army with a view to regaining powerful places in the imperial court.

With the rising of the sun on 16 May 218, the fourteen-year-old Elagabalus, son of Soemias, was proclaimed emperor in the camp of legion III Gallica at Raphanaea, ninety miles south of Antioch. All three ladies were present, having made arrangements in advance. Macrinus reacted promptly; his praetorian prefect, Julianus, tried to capture III Gallica's camp with a scratch force. Julianus failed and fled to the camp of II Parthica at Apamea. Instead of rising to Julianus's call, the men of II Parthica beheaded him. When Macrinus later came to the camp to try to gain their support, they first accepted a handsome donative and then showed him Julianus's head on a spear, proving that they were for Elagabalus. The commanding officer of II Gallica at the time was P. Valerius Comazon, whom Elagabalus would shortly name praetorian prefect.

Rebuffed by II Parthica, Macrinus returned to Antioch and organized such forces as he could lay his hands on. Since the troops favoring Elagabalus were preparing to move against Antioch, there was not enough time to bring south the legions at

Zeugma and Samosata, Zeugma being 120 miles away and Samosata much farther. So, inevitably, the praetorians made up the bulk of the small army Macrinus led southward to meet Elagabalus. One can estimate that there were eight cohorts of the guard with support from auxiliaries, including the Moroccan troops from Macrinus's homeland—a force of possibly nine thousand men. Some twenty-four miles south of Antioch, they met and engaged Elagabalus's troops, which consisted of two legions and auxiliaries, about eleven thousand men. In a day-long battle in June, the praetorians, although outnumbered, were more than holding their own until Macrinus disappeared from the field. He probably sensed a standoff and may have gone north in the hope of getting reinforcements. The praetorians, believing their leader either dead or in flight, succumbed to the appeals of the enemy. The praetorians were promised that they would be continued as the guard of the new emperor and were undoubtedly given a handsome donative. Thus ended a costly battle between two Roman armies to determine whether a Moroccan or a Syrian would rule in Rome.[6]

Macrinus, having received the bad news from the south, attempted to escape in disguise and get to Rome. He was captured and killed in Turkey on the 8th of July.

Three

Fano and Milvian Bridge

With Elagabalus, the praetorians found themselves involved for the third time with a teenage emperor. Furthermore, Elagabalus came to them with the three aggressive ladies: Maesa, the emperor's grandmother; Soemias, his mother; and Mamaea, his aunt, whose nine-year-old son, Alexander, was destined to be emperor four years hence. The guard, having spent some five years away from Rome and having fought several campaigns, was probably delighted to escort this group back to the capital city. There the praetorian prefects were Comazon, former commander of II Parthica, and Antiochianus.

Elagabalus did not make a favorable impression in Rome. Hereditary priest of the god Baal of Emesia, the young emperor insisted on wearing priestly robes and dancing before the temple of the Emesan deity which he had established in Rome. Although Eastern religions were no surprise to the populace, the strange behavior of their emperor was startling. Elagabalus also violated sensitivities by marrying one of the vestal virgins, divorcing her, and then marrying her again. Pages of history are devoted to his vastly expensive and public debauchery. It appears that he assembled large numbers of prostitutes and catamites, addressed them as praetorians, and gave them donatives. He also tried to emulate Nero in his most lascivious activities. He instituted human sacrifice and killed the children of many prominent Romans.

Elagabalus's strange activities distressed his wise grandmother, who saw trouble coming. She persuaded her grandson to adopt his cousin Alexander as heir presumptive in 221. He soon regretted this action, for Alexander was being educated by scholars who were instructing him in some of the arts needed by an emperor. Alexander also refused to participate in his cousin's strange cult activities, which did not please the emperor. Feeling menaced, Elagabalus asked the senate to demote his cousin Alexander from caesar, the rank which he himself had put forward and which carried with it the concept of heir apparent. The Senate heard the request in silence, after which Elagabalus is reported to have ordered all members to leave Rome at once. When one senator by the name of Sabinus failed to obey promptly, the emperor called aside a centurion and ordered him in a low voice to kill him. The centurion, however, was somewhat deaf and mistook the order. Thinking that he had been ordered to escort Sabinus out of Rome, he did just that, much to the annoyance of the emperor.

Elagabalus, having dismissed the senate and being very unpopular with both the castra and the public at large, decided to have Alexander murdered. After his several efforts, most of them by the use of poison, had been blocked by his palace-wise grandmother, he gave a direct order to the praetorian cohort then on palace duty to proceed to the garden where Alexander happened to be and execute him. The prefect in charge, Antiochianus, countermanded the order and withdrew the cohort to the castra. Threatened and without a protecting guard, Elagabalus proceeded with some of his entourage to the castra, pressing Alexander to ride with him as a shield against possible mob violence. Admitted to the castra, he spent the night in the temple of Mars at the center of the castra, where the standards of the cohorts were kept. The following morning, he issued orders through his entourage for the execution of all supporters of Alexander. The guard, which was highly contemptuous of Elagabalus and strongly in favor of Alexander, not only failed to carry out these orders, but executed Elagabalus instead.[1]

Having proclaimed Alexander emperor, the guard escorted him back to the palace. The senate, as soon as it could be assembled, endorsed his selection[2] with enthusiasm and ordered removal of the name of Elagabalus from all monuments and inscriptions. On 13 March 222, the praetorians earned the thanks of the senate and people of Rome for disposing of the most dissolute, corrupt, and venal of all the emperors Rome was to see.

Alexander was thirteen years old when he became emperor. Thus for the fourth time the praetorians had a teenage ruler. This time, however, the situation was different. Alexander was the choice of the senate, the people, and the guard itself. He was, however, largely under the control of his grandmother, Maesa, and, after her death, his mother, Mamaea.

The first eight years of this emperor's reign did not involve any foreign duty for the praetorians. Their prefects included two famous jurists. One was Julius Paulus, who was executed A.D. 235, the year in which the next emperor, Maximinus, came to power. The other and more famous jurist was Domitius Ulpianus, a native of Tyre who had done his greatest work during the rule of Caracalla. Elagabalus had banished Ulpianus, but he was brought back during Alexander's time.

To maintain a good relationship with the castra, the palace made three different donatives. To maintain a good standing with the senate, it was careful to get senate approval whenever new praetorian prefects were named. Other prefects during Alexander's reign were M. Attius Cornelianus, who was appointed about 230 and was executed when Maximinus took over control, and C. Furius Sabinus Aquila Timesitheus, who had been *procurator* in Palestine.

One problem that arose for the castra before the praetorians went off to the wars in 231 centered on Alexander's wife, who had been selected for him by his mother, Mamaea. Mamaea soon discovered that there could be only one empress and that Alexander's new wife had been a mistake. Although Alexander loved her, she was expelled from the palace. Her father, Seius Caesar, was upset by this treatment of his daughter and went to the castra for help. Mamaea proved to be the more powerful. She had the father executed and the daughter exiled to Libya.

War having broken out in the East and Rome's interests being subverted by Persia, an army of considerable size was organized in 230 under the management of Julius Flavianus, a leading praetorian prefect. The following year, the praetorians moved out with the rest of the army and crossed over to Antioch. Alexander's quite sizeable forces were organized into three columns to invade Mesopotamia — one on the north to advance westward, crossing the Euphrates at Melitene; one on the south to strike northeast from the area of Ctesiphon; and a third in the center, with Alexander at its head and the praetorians conspicuous among the troops, to drive westward from the vicinity of Palmyra. The northern column seems to have met with some success, but the southern column was defeated and lost many men. The column in the center, for unexplained reasons, made no advance but stayed in place near Palmyra with the emperor and his mother.[3]

The troops were disgruntled by the mismanagement of the campaign, so another handsome donative came from the emperor, who moved his headquarters to Antioch. The Persians must have also suffered damage, for they remained quiescent for some time. Alexander's peaceful residence in Antioch, however, was brought to an end by outbreaks of fighting on both the Rhine and the Danube. Both frontiers were partly overrun. With a considerable part of his army, Alexander moved to the Rhine front in an attempt to get things in hand. He placed a former tribune of the praetorians, G. Julius Verus Maximinus, in charge of training. Maximinus, whose duties went considerably beyond training, was very popular with the army, being viewed as a successful soldier whereas Alexander was not. An uprising took place and all the troops, including the emperor's guards, went over to Maximinus, whom the army promptly proclaimed emperor. Maximinus then dispatched several centurions to Alexander's quarters near Mainz, where they killed Alexander, his mother, and two praetorian prefects.

The date of Alexander's death was probably 22 March 235. For the next three years Roman history was markedly confused. Having disposed of Alexander, Maximinus proceeded to conduct a successful campaign against the Germans. He built a bridge over the Rhine near Mainz and drove deep into the German lands, subsequently reporting his triumph to the senate. M. Aedinus Julianus may well have been the field praetorian prefect with the cohorts in Germany. If so, here was another example of a praetorian prefect having previously served as prefect of Egypt. In Rome, P. Aelius Vitalianus was the prefect;

he represented Maximinus and was in command of the cohorts that remained there.

Having gotten the German situation under control, Maximinus moved on to the Danube front to prepare for a major offensive in the spring. His plans, however, were disrupted when a revolt broke out in Africa. N. Antonius Gordianus Sempronianus, the eighty-year-old proconsul there, was proclaimed emperor by a large body of men who disliked Maximinus. Gordian, who assumed power on 1 March 238, set up headquarters in Carthage and immediately got off dispatches to the senate and the provincial governors explaining his action. The senators were delighted with this report, having confirmed Maximinus with great reluctance. They at once deposed Maximinus and recognized Gordian as emperor. Vitalianus, Maximinus's powerful praetorian prefect in Rome, was killed by Gordian's agents who, not surprisingly, announced a major donative for the guardsmen immediately thereafter.

Back in Africa, things were not going according to plan. The legion at Lambaesis remained loyal to Maximinus and advanced on Carthage. Gordian's son led forth a small army on 22 March and was defeated, losing his life on the battlefield. His father, learning of the disaster, killed himself. Thus in less than a month the uprising was over and both Gordian I and Gordian II were dead.

The senate in Rome now found itself in an unenviable position. The emperor they recognized was dead and the one they had deposed would soon be marching on Rome to put things to rights. Those cohorts of the guard that were in the castra seemed restive, for they had taken a liking to the thirteen-year-old grandson of Gordian I who was living with his mother in Rome.

After due consideration, the senate named two of its own members as co-emperors, M. Claudius Pupienus Maximus and D. Caelius Calvinus Balbinus. Maximus had a good military reputation and had served as prefect of the city. Balbinus had been a proconsul in Asia. To placate the praetorians, who were not pleased with this decision, the senate gave young Gordian the rank of caesar, a title which by this time had come to mean an emperor's subordinate co-ruler and presumptive heir.

Maximus organized an army and set forth to meet the advancing Maximinus, who had progressed as far as Aquileia in northeastern Italy on the Gulf of Venice. Here Maximinus was bogged down, for the city refused to surrender and he could not take it by storm. He was personally in a bad way. He had executed some of his officers, apparently willfully, and had alienated most of his troops because of indiscriminately harsh treatment. For help, he summoned II Parthica, the legion from Albano. The legionnaires, however, arrived already ill-disposed toward him. Some of them rushed his tent, killing him, his son, and the praetorian prefect, probably Julianus, who was with him at the time.

Maximus arrived on the scene in time to participate in general rejoicing and to announce a donative. He sent the legions to their regular stations and returned to Rome with the praetorians. Once there, these troops promptly took on the attitude of their peers, almost all of whom held Maximus and Balbinus in low esteem.

Pinarius Valens, an old friend of Maximus, was made praetorian prefect. Despite his fine military record, which included successful campaigns on both the Rhine and Danube fronts, he does not seem to have been able to bring the troops to a favorable attitude toward Maximus.

The attitude of the praetorians had hardened because of an incident that took place in Rome while Maximus was away in the north. Two of their number were at the senate gate watching proceedings when they appeared to have advanced too far into the chamber. There they had been stabbed to death by two senators. General rioting took place, during which the populace made an assault on the castra. Although few in number— most of their colleagues being in the north with Maximus—the praetorians were veteran soldiers and put up an effective defense. They launched several sallies and drove the attackers back. When the attackers cut off the water supply to the barracks, the praetorians went over to the offensive, aggressively pursuing their enemies through the streets, finally burning many of them out of the homes in which they had taken refuge. Before order could be restored, some important sections of Rome had been leveled.[4]

Although the situation seemed to have quieted after the return of Maximus with the bulk of the praetorians, dislike of the two emperors by the soldiers at the castra increased. About 8 July 238, a body of praetorians attacked the palace and seized and killed the two emperors and their prefect Valens. Immediately thereafter they took Caesar Gordian to the castra and proclaimed him emperor. Apparently the senate had no choice but to confirm their actions. Thus the guard proclaimed their fifth and last teenage emperor.

The *Augustan History* devotes pages of praise to Maximus and Balbinus. Without mentioning the murder of the two unarmed praetorians by senators, it describes the rioting and the attack on the castra and goes on to report that a greater part of the city was ruined as a result of the praetorian counterattack, which is highly questionable. The senate, in praising Maximus, is quoted as dismissing the death of Maximinus as the fate of emperors put in power by fools. As Maximinus had been placed in power by the army, the praetorians took this as an insult to all soldiers. The history does touch, but only lightly, on the bungling of the two emperors, each fearing that the other was trying to gain sole power. As a result of this bungling, there were no German guards to protect them when the enraged praetorians seized them. The account concludes with the statement that never was there anyone braver than Maximus or kinder than Balbinus.

Herodian, who may have been a senator himself, expresses the senatorial dislike of the guard even more vigorously. He argues that the soldiers were seething with anger because the two emperors had been senators and had been selected by the senate. Describing their killing, he goes into great detail about torture and mutilation and the final abandonment of the bodies in the street, but makes no comment and gives no details on the killing of the praetorians.

Neither source mentions what happened, if anything, to the killers of the two praetorians at the senate entrance. Also significant is the failure of either to tell how many praetorians were killed by the mob that attacked the castra. This attack appears to have taken place over a period of several days and must have been well organized and skillfully led. The cutting off of the water supply was a difficult task and not the work of an ill-led mob. It is also hard to understand why the emperor Balbinus made no effective effort to halt the attack on the castra. Possibly he believed that the attack might be successful, as the castra at this time was occupied mainly by new recruits, old soldiers awaiting discharge, and the sick or wounded.

When the main body of the praetorians returned to Rome, they were without doubt enraged to find out about the murders at the senate, the attack on their base, and the killing of many of their comrades. Such may well have been the underlying cause for the killing of the two senator-emperors.

A final comment on the two classical sources: Neither admits that the one-year rule of the two senators was an unhappy time for Rome nor that the succeeding emperor, Gordian III, provided a much better rule. Gordian III was a praetorian selection.

The first guard prefect appointed by Gordian III was Domitius, who had helped engineer the overthrow of Maximus and Balbinus. By A.D. 241 he had been replaced by Timesitheus and G. Julius Priscus. Priscus was the brother of the future emperor Philip, but he himself did not leave a notable record. Furius Sabinus Aquila Timesitheus, on the other hand, was one of the greatest of the praetorian prefects. A soldier of distinction, he was *procurator* in Gaul in the spring of 241. That year, Gordian married Timesitheus's daughter, Tranquillina, and appointed his father-in-law praetorian prefect.

Early in the reign of Gordian III, a revolt occurred in Africa that was put down with little difficulty, but shortly thereafter a serious situation arose. The Persians, under their new king, Sapor I, broke into the empire, crossing the Euphrates and even threatening Antioch itself. In response, Timesitheus put together a large and well-organized army, including the bulk of the guard. Gordian then took the field, with Timesitheus as his troop commander, marching through Moesia and Thrace and then crossing the Hellespont. While following this course he engaged and defeated Goths and others who were menacing from north of the Danube. Arriving in the Antioch area, the Roman army inflicted a smashing defeat on the Persians, clearing them from Carrhae and Nisibus. After the reconquest of northern Mesopotamia, Gordian and Timesitheus led the army south, with Ctesiphon as the objective. Unfortunately at this juncture Timesitheus died, apparently of dysentery.

Historians who disagree on many things all seem to admire and praise Timesitheus. He not only had the following of his praetorians but was relied upon by the young emperor to handle most of the affairs of the empire. This he did well, by all accounts, and he did not fatten his own purse. When he died, he left his entire fortune to the state. The *Augustan History* calls Timesitheus an erudite man of great eloquence.[5]

Upon Timesitheus's death, Gordian unwisely appointed Marcus Julius Philippus as praetorian prefect and field commander. At about the same time, he appointed as a second prefect in the field a relative, Maecius Gordianus, a man who remained loyal to the emperor but not effectively so. Philippus, whose brother Priscus was praetorian prefect back in Rome, was an Arab by birth, an effective soldier, and very ambitious. Soon after gaining the command position, Philippus had himself named co-emperor and shortly thereafter Gordian was killed. There seems to be little question that Gordian's death was arranged by Philippus, who now became the emperor Philip. Philip then brought the war to a close and proceeded with the guard to Rome. He sent dispatches to Rome praising Gordian and from this time forward always called him divine.

Marcus Julius Philippus, praetorian prefect appointed by Gordian in 243. In 244 he became emperor and ruled until 249, when he was killed in battle by the next emperor, Caius Messius Quintus Decius.

The praetorians returned to the castra with every reason to count on a pleasurable and influential time in the capital. The emperor was a creation of the army and a former praetorian prefect. His brother, Priscus, continued as the praetorian prefect. Praetorian expectations were, however, soon disappointed, for troubles broke out on the Danube again, and Philip waged a rather long but successful campaign there. In 248, Philip returned to Rome with his praetorians and celebrated in the spring with much pomp and magnificence the last secular games Rome was to see.

The following year, the Danube front unraveled again with both revolts and usurpations taking place. Philip selected Caius Messius Quintus Decius, an experienced commander, to quell the troubles. Decius instead had himself proclaimed emperor as soon as he had control of the troops, whereupon Philip put together an army including some of the guard and moved to attack Decius. The two armies met near Verona. Philip lost both the battle and his life. When the news reached Rome, that portion of the guard that had remained in the city executed Philip's son, who had been named caesar by his father.

Decius had but a few months to enjoy Rome before the Danube front was again shattered, requiring him to lead such troops as he could gather to rectify the situation. An initial defeat at the hands of the Goths forced him to retreat. He regrouped, however, and in a series of engagements forced the Goths to withdraw and give up much of their plunder.

The Roman army in 251 suffered a decisive defeat at Abrittus in central Dobruja, not far from present-day Constanta on the Black Sea. Here both Decius and his son lost their lives.

In Rome, the senate named Decius's surviving son, Hostilianus, emperor. The more experienced Caius Vibius Trebonianus Gallus was named co-emperor and guardian. Hostilianus soon died of the plague and Gallus, the choice of the troops in Moesia, found himself trying to make peace with the Goths. Then Aemilianus, who commanded Roman troops on the Danube, claimed the purple for himself and defeated Gallus's forces in 253, killing both Gallus and his son. Four months later, Aemilianus's army turned on its leader at Spoleto and killed him. This cleared the way for Publius Licinius Valerian, a man who had held important military and civilian posts under both Decius and Gallus.

Historical records of the reigns of Philip, Decius, and Gallus are sparse, and no record has been found of the activities of the guard or the appointment of praetorian prefects. It may be assumed, however, that at least a portion of the guard was at Verona when Philip was defeated, and some of the guard fought beside Decius during his unfortunate campaign against the Goths.

During the period 253 to 268, when Valerian and Gallienus ruled, records are a bit more complete. It was a busy time for both the guard and its prefects. Valerian was proclaimed by the troops of Raetia when he was there on a mission for the emperor Gallus. In his sixties, a man of distinction and a senator, Valerian was reluctant to take on the emperor's mantle. But by the time he got back to Rome, both Gallus and Aemilianus were dead, and he accepted the task of trying to reunite the empire. He appointed his son, Publius Licinius Egnatius Gallienus, co-emperor and assigned him the wars in Europe. He himself set out for the East to put things in order. Gallienus, who had his headquarters at Treves, entrusted his forces to his general, Posthumus, who conducted several successful campaigns but failed to hold the Germans in check. A large force of the Alemanni crossed the Danube and advanced into Italy as far as Ravenna with obvious intent to plunder Rome itself.

Faced with this critical situation, the senate, not known for excessive friendliness toward the guard, provided for rapid recruitment to bring the guard up to full strength. New troops were needed to replace those cohorts away in Gaul or in the East with the two emperors. The guard, presumably reinforced with some elements of the city troops, did not wait for the Alemanni to appear before the gates; they sallied forth at a strength of possibly eleven thousand to intercept the invaders in their advance southward. Success came to the guard, and the invaders were promptly driven out of Italy and back to their homeland. This very creditable performance must have given the guard a brief but desirable popularity in the city.

60

Valerian, engaging the Persians in Syria, had initial success, clearing Antioch and other eastern areas of Persian control. His praetorian prefect, Ballista, not only controlled the praetorians but also was the general in command of Valerian's army.

Unfortunately the emperor, who failed to take precautions for his own safety, was captured by the Persians and died in captivity some time later. The prefect Successianus was captured with him. Ballista tried to set up an emperor of his own choice; he failed and was killed in battle defending Macrianus, his candidate. The *Augustan History* mentions three other praetorian prefects during Valerian's rule. Mulvius Gallicanus and Ablavius Murena were most likely in command of the guard in Rome itself, as the *History* quotes letters to them from Valerian. It is quite possible that one or both of them led the guard out of Rome to defeat the Alemanni. Baebius Macer is mentioned as prefect at the time when Valerian adopted the future emperor Aurelian as his son and presumably his successor. No other mention of Macer has come to light.[6]

Valerian's son, Publius Licinius Egnatius Gallienus, seems to have felt little sorrow at his father's capture and subsequent death. He ruled as sole emperor from 260 to 268 and did not do much to preserve the empire. Field commanders did what they could without the emperor's active participation, but everywhere, on the Danube, on the Rhine, and in the East, things went badly. Despite his having a capable praetorian prefect, L. Petronius Taurus Volusianus, Gallienus was disliked in Rome and had only slight support when he faced an uprising of his generals. The other praetorian prefect, Aurelius Heraclianus, organized the plot in which two emperors-to-be, Claudius II and Aurelian, participated. The murder took place outside Milan, where Gallienus had taken some troops to put down one of the frequent uprisings. The legions, if not the guard, were upset by this action, but the promise of twenty gold pieces for each man seems to have assuaged their discontent.

Two years later, in 270, the praetorians were again called on to save Rome from the Alemanni. The then emperor Aurelian was in Pannonia. Having conducted a successful repulse of the Vandals, he soon learned that the Alemanni, moving rapidly, had invaded Italy with the obvious objective of looting Rome. The situation was serious, since most of the praetorians were in Pannonia with Aurelian and there were no forces to repel the invaders. Taking only the praetorian cohorts and some auxiliary troops, and instructing the slower moving legions to follow as fast as possible, Aurelian, by forced marches, caught up with the Alemanni at Placenta. There he suffered a reverse but continued to throw his troops against the invaders and finally won two major victories, one at Fano and the other near Pavia. The Alemanni, much weakened, were again driven out of Italy. Undoubtedly men who had repulsed the Alemanni only fifteen years earlier were participants in this victory. Thus twice in a relatively short period of time, the praetorians had saved the city of Rome from destruction by barbarians.

During Aurelian's reign, the castra received an important physical reinforcement. Aurelian, who was highly conscious of the peril for Rome should the barbarians reach the city, undertook the construction of a new, larger, and longer wall around the expanded city. This new wall used the east and north walls of the castra and part of the south wall as part of the defensive works of Rome.

Originally built in the time of Tiberius, the castra wall was only twelve to fourteen feet high. Aurelian increased the height to some forty feet. At the time of this writing the wall still stands. The beauty and neatness of the original brick facing contrasts markedly with the less precise work of Aurelian's time.

History records the names of two of Aurelian's praetorian prefects, both men of ability. Julius Placidianus, who was commanding troops in Gaul when Aurelian came to power, was highly regarded by the emperor; he and the emperor had served as consuls at the same time.[7] The other prefect was Moesius Gallicanus. It was he who in 275 presented Tacitus to the troops for their approval. Upon the assassination of Aurelian, the senate selected Tacitus, but he could not rule safely as emperor until so named by the troops. It is unclear whether this presentaton by Gallicanus took place in Rome at the castra, or in Thrace. In any event, after having been promised a handsome donative, the troops accepted the recommendation of the praetorian prefect and hailed Marcus Claudius Tacitus as emperor.

Another matter that remains unclear is the participation of the praetorians themselves in the successful campaign of Aurelian against Palmyra in 272. One can be sure, however, that they did participate in the triumph that was celebrated in Rome. In that great procession Zenobia, the captured queen of Palmyra, had to march in golden chains while arrayed in masses of jewelry. Aurelian, who was known for his strictness, was generous to Zenobia. A woman of great style, Zenobia was of pure Macedonian stock, as was Cleopatra. She was so well thought of in Rome that two of her sons were eventually made rulers of minor kingdoms. She ended her days living in a handsome estate outside Rome.

During the period 275 to 284, six emperors reigned, all beset with foreign wars. There was much shifting around of praetorian prefects. Tacitus kept Gallicanus, who had more or less sponsored him, and also appointed Capito for the command in Rome itself.[8] Capito was kept on by the next emperor, Marcus Aurelius Probus, who also appointed, apparently as his praetorian prefect and field commander, Marcus Aurelius Carus. Carus successfully conducted the campaign against the Persians and captured the capital, Ctesiphon. Shortly thereafter, the troops in Ratia and Noricum proclaimed Carus emperor. Hearing this, troops on their way with Probus to the East for another Persian campaign revolted and killed him. Apparently the praetorian cohorts with Probus preferred Carus as emperor to the man who had appointed him.

Praetorian cohorts are presumed to have been used by Aurelian in his capture of Palmyra and its queen, Zenobia (right). Zenobia was of Macedonian stock and distantly related to Cleopatra (left).

Carus, the fourth and last praetorian prefect to become emperor, appointed as his prefects M. Flavius Aper and Tiberius Claudius Aurelius Aristobulis. Carus's campaign against the Persians went well, but unfortunately he died the next year in Mesopotamia. His son, Numerian, then took over command of the troops but died promptly under mysterious circumstances. A great assembly of the troops was held, with Aper and Diocletian on the stand. Diocletian, then commander of the household troops, accused Aper of murdering Numerian, drew his sword, and killed him. The troops then proclaimed Diocletian emperor.

The next nineteen years were to be dominated by this one man, D. Aurelius Diocletian, whose reign was to continue until he retired in 305. His first praetorian prefect was the same Aristobulis who had been named prefect by Carus in 282. Africanus Hannibalianus is mentioned as prefect in 296, but the most famous of Diocletian's prefects was Julius Asclepiodotus, who held the position from 285 to 297. It was he who led the army that invaded Britain in 296, defeated the pretender to the throne, Allectus, and restored Britain to the empire of Diocletian. Asclepiodotus commanded not only the troops but also the fleet that took his army to Britain, one of the few occasions when a praetorian prefect is known to have had a sea command. He burned the ships as soon as he was established ashore, no doubt to show that there would be no turning back. It is possible that his invasion force included some of the praetorians.

Perhaps the most dramatic campaign of the praetorian cohorts during this period was in Africa. Diocletian had named as junior co-emperor Marcus Aurelius Valerius Maximian, a good troop commander. In 288, when the emperor ordered him to put down revolts in North Africa, Maximian assembled a task force built around several cohorts of praetorians, including elements of three legions and some auxiliary troops. Crossing at Gibraltar, he marched his troops all the way to Carthage, destroying disloyal elements along the way. He made a triumphal entrance into Carthage as the restorer of the Roman Empire in North Africa.

Rome's praetorians did not fare well, however, during the latter part of Diocletian's reign, for this emperor had a distrust of the guard. By the date of his retirement, he had eliminated many of its privileges, reduced the strength of the cohorts, and attempted to relegate the guard to the status of a Roman garrison.

The army as a whole also suffered radical changes during Diocletian's time. Existing legions were reduced in size, and a number of new small ones were created. To back up the frontier troops, a central reserve of cavalry was set up under the direct command of the emperor. One reason for the reduction in size and effectiveness of the legions was the fear that several strong legions would band together and name their own emperor, as they had often done before in alliance with the praetorians. The reduced effectiveness of both the legions and the guard may have made life more agreeable for the emperor, but it certainly made the defense of the empire more difficult.

The empire itself was becoming a rather confused state, for Diocletian had established a structure of two emperors, each having a caesar under him ready to take his place. When Diocletian retired and Maximian reluctantly did likewise, the system fell apart; at one time there were six ruling emperors,[9] each with his own capital and praetorian prefect acting as commander or prime minister.

The fortunes of the guard were greatly improved when Marcus Aurelius Maxentius, the son of Maximian, seized power in Rome. Flavius Valerius Severus had been appointed emperor for Italy and had his headquarters not in Rome, but at Milan. The guard particularly disliked Severus, for he carried on Diocletian's program of suppression. On 28 October 306, under the leadership of the praetorian prefect Anulius, the citizens of Rome revolted and killed Severus's representatives there. Severus assembled an army and moved against Maxentius's Rome, but on arrival at the walls of the city, his troops showed an inclination to favor Maxentius. Severus retreated to Ravenna.

Meanwhile, Maximian had come out of retirement and taken command of a force to attack Ravenna. For a time Severus defended the city, but he finally succumbed to the blandishments of Maximian, surrendered the city, and was taken as an honored prisoner to Rome.

In 307, the emperor who had sponsored Severus, Caius Galerius Valerius Maximinianus, led an army to Italy to reestablish Severus. On reaching the walls of Rome, Galerius had no better fortune than Severus; he had to quickly withdraw from Italy to avoid losing his entire army by desertion. Severus, who was still prisoner in Rome, was then executed.

Maxentius was keenly aware of the importance of the praetorians. He promptly restored their old privileges and brought the cohorts up to full strength, possibly to an overstrength. This special favoring of the guard proved to be wise, for when Maxentius's father, Maximian, tired of playing the part of deputy emperor and made an effort to take back the primary position, it was the guard that foiled him. Maxentius went in person to the castra and strongly presented his case to the praetorians, who firmly supported him. Maximian fled to the court of his son-in-law, Constantine, at Arles. Constantine was the gifted and ambitious son of the emperor Constantius I and St. Helena. When his father died in York in 306, he was proclaimed emperor by the troops in Britain. Like his father, he was an excellent soldier. Maximian made the mistake of trying to take over while Constantine was away at the frontier. Upon his return, Constantine suppressed the small uprising and pursued Maximian to Marseilles, where he permitted the old emperor to commit suicide.

By the year 312, Maxentius had convinced himself that there should be only one emperor—Maxentius. He had disposed easily of a small uprising in Africa, and, believing his part of the empire secure, he started to organize an army for the invasion of Gaul. But in Gaul Constantine had reached a similar conclusion, that there should be only one emperor. Quicker off the mark, he invaded Italy before Maxentius could complete his preparations.

Maxentius was initially confident that his general, Ruricius Pompeianus, could handle the invading forces. His confidence, however, was short-lived. Maxentius's troops were badly beaten, first near Turin and later near Verona. Pompeianus lost his life, and the army in northern Italy either was forced to surrender or voluntarily went over to Constantine.

Maxentius was now in a critical situation, for all he had left for the defense of Rome were the praetorian guard, the urban cohorts, and certain auxiliary troops. He probably had ten praetorian and two urban 1,000-man cohorts, but of these, 1,000 would have been either away on special duty, on leave, or sick.[10] To this 11,000 could be added some 4,000 auxiliary troops, mainly Moorish and Numidian light cavalry. Although the units in the army of Constantine are not known, they can be assumed to have included detachments from the legions of the army of the Rhine and, for auxiliaries, cavalry mounted on the superior horses of Gaul. All told, he probably had under command in Gaul and on the Rhine some 75,000 men. At least half of these, however, had to remain in place to hold the frontiers.[11] Furthermore, after his two victories in the north of Italy he may have had no more than 30,000 effectives, and five thousand soldiers would have been needed to keep an eye on the defeated troops of Maxentius. Thus, for the attack on Rome, Constantine would have had about 25,000 men, some 10,000 more than Maxentius was able to marshal for its defense.

An engagement between the two forces may have occurred on 16 October 312. If there was such a preliminary brush, the result was probably favorable to the praetorians. The decisive battle took place the following day near Saxa Rubra (Red Rocks) north of Rome. Maxentius drew up his troops on the far side of the Tiber with the river behind him. The crossing was made over the Milvian Bridge which, though much rebuilt, still stands. He placed the praetorians and his command post in the center, with the auxiliary troops on the flanks.

Constantine used a similar formation, with the cavalry on the two flanks and his legionary cohorts in the center. Constan-

The Greek chi *and* rho *as a monogram for Christ depicted on a coin issued by Constantine about 333. At the battle of Milvian Bridge in 312 Constantine required all his troops to paint the* Christos *on their shields.*

67

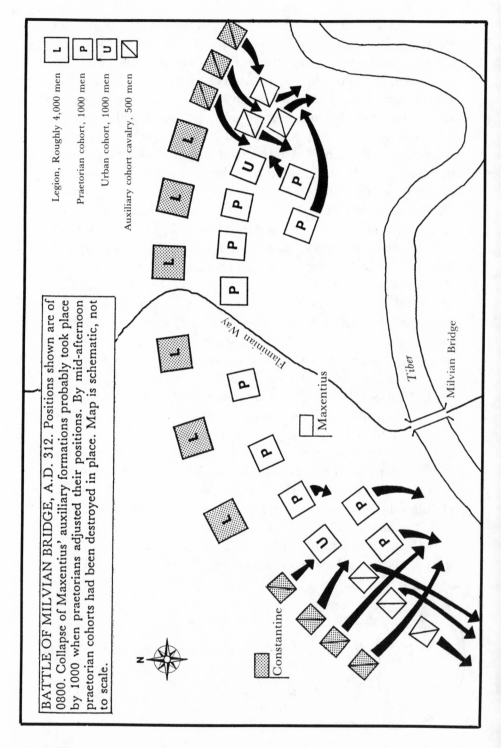

BATTLE OF MILVIAN BRIDGE, A.D. 312. Positions shown are of 0800. Collapse of Maxentius' auxiliary formations probably took place by 1000 when praetorians adjusted their positions. By mid-afternoon praetorian cohorts had been destroyed in place. Map is schematic, not to scale.

Legion, Roughly 4,000 men

Praetorian cohort, 1000 men

Urban cohort, 1000 men

Auxiliary cohort cavalry, 500 men

Flaminian Way

Maxentius

Constantine

Tiber

Milvian Bridge

tine, however, took personal command of the cavalry on one of the flanks. On the previous day, all his troops had been ordered to inscribe on their shields the monogram XP, the *Christos*. The two Greek letters *chi* and *rho* are the first two letters of the Greek word for Christ. The X and P monogram, when read as Latin characters, could stand for *pax,* or *peace,* although this certainly was not Constantine's intent on that day. Constantine had not yet become a Christian, but undoubtedly he believed in the psychological advantage of this unifying symbol.

The engagement opened with a violent and successful attack by the Gallic cavalry under the personal command of Constantine. The light cavalry of Maxentius was driven from the field, leaving one flank of the praetorians exposed. An assault against the other flank by Constantine's cavalry was equally successful, and the praetorians found themselves fighting on three fronts. Many of Maxentius's auxiliaries sought to flee the field over the Milvian Bridge. Maxentius, seeing things going badly, tried to cross the bridge himself to get back to Rome. The pressure of the mob on the bridge was so great, however, that the emperor was forced over the parapet. His heavy armor weighed him down and he drowned almost unnoticed by the fleeing troops. His body was not found until the next day.

The praetorians, however, did not retreat. The reserve cohorts on the right and left turned to secure the praetorian flanks on the Tiber. Assuming a half moon formation, they continued the battle without the emperor. They had no illusions about their fate should they be defeated, for Constantine had made it clear that the praetorians were to exist no longer.

Fighting with skill and great courage, the praetorians held their position for many hours, but in the end were overcome by superior numbers. Observers noted, however, that their bodies were found in almost the exact positions that had been assigned at the beginning of the battle. There had been no retreat. Almost to a man, the praetorians died on the battlefield of Saxa Rubra.[12]

***

The victorious Constantine abolished not only the guard but also the city cohorts and the watch. The inner walls of the castra praetoria were torn down. (The outer walls had to be maintained as they were part of the defenses of Rome.) The few surviving praetorians were dispatched to the frontiers to become fillers for understrength legions.

Thus ended the praetorian guard, and with its demise ended a truly imperial Rome. The title "praetorian prefect" was continued, but the prefects of the later empire were divorced from military command and served as administrators, governors of provinces, or as ministers to future emperors. Bereft of troops to defend it, and without the presence of an emperor, Rome lost its leadership in an empire that still called itself Roman but was ruled from Constantinople. The empty castra echoed the hollowness of the senate's claim to a continuing power. Before long, another senate was set up in Constantinople, thus destroying any lingering illusion.

Part Two

The Imperial Legions

Four

The Nature of the Imperial Legions

Profiting from the tactical and organizational genius of Caesar, Anthony, and their predecessors, the emperor Augustus (27 B.C.-A.D. 14) established a standing army of twenty-eight legions. This army, supported by auxiliary troops, was to remain unchanged in basic essentials for almost three centuries.

Until the time of Augustus, legions had been recruited as needed and subsequently disbanded. The Augustan legion was, on the other hand, a permanent military unit made up entirely of Roman citizens who could retire normally after twenty years' service. On retirement, the soldiers received from the emperor grants of money or land or both and usually lifetime exemption from taxation for themselves and their wives.[1]

Legion commanders were selected by the emperor and were considered his personal representatives. They were titled *legatus,* and were usually young men of the senatorial class whose military experience was probably limited to serving on the staff of another legion commander. After a couple of years as a *legatus,* a man usually went on to another important post, such as commanding an army or governing a province. Most were, or became, senators, and at least eight became emperors. Legion command was considered more an executive and leadership position than one involving a profound knowledge of tactics and strategy. The commander had a staff of six tribunes, one of whom was also of the senatorial class and destined himself to command a legion. The other five were probably of the equestrian class, had experience with auxiliary troops, and would probably go on to be commanders of important auxiliary cohorts. All six tribunes handled administrative matters for the legion, while the sixty centurions exercised command, directly subordinate to the *legatus*. Each of the ten cohorts that made up the legion was, in combat, under the command of a senior centurion.

The centurions were the life and survival of the legion. They were professional soldiers, probably rose from the ranks, and were charged with training, discipline, command in combat, and the general morale and well-being of the legion. Each normally commanded a century. Obviously, in early history, the century had a hundred men, but this was soon reduced to eighty and so remained. The centurion carried a staff or swagger stick of grape vine as the symbol of his office and used it on occasion to beat recalcitrant soldiers. His pay during the Augustan period was 3,750 denarii per year, compared to 225 denarii for new recruits. His authority was almost limitless. He created officers junior to himself, personally conducted training, and awarded leaves of absence at his own discretion. This discretion included a payment to the centurion by the man going on leave. This unwise practice was eliminated by the emperor Otho in 69. The centurion's pay was then increased by an equivalent amount.

The senior centurion in the legion was known as the *primus pilus* and was the tactical commander. He was very well paid, receiving, in the time of Augustus, four times the pay of other centurions. Emperors made sure that the *primus pilus* was protected against inflation. By the time of the emperor Domitian (81-96), he was receiving 20,000 denarii, as compared to the 15,000 denarii of sixty years earlier. Centurions moved from legion to legion in accordance with their own desires or the needs of the army and often went on to higher civilian and military jobs. As an example, P. Anicius Maximus, *primus pilus* of Legion XII Fulminata in Syria about 70, became camp prefect (camp commander) for II Augusta in Britain and then camp prefect in Egypt for two legions in a joint camp at Nicopolis,[2] just east of Alexandria.

The training in a legion was continuous, and most of the soldiers were professional and served for at least twenty years. Training for combat was conducted with double-weight swords,

In the hot springs of this imposing public bath at Aquae Sulis, Legionnaires found refuge from the cold of Northern Britian. Aquae Sulis was a small walled town in the sheltered Avon Valley, the site of modern Bath.

shields, and spears and was very realistic, including the construction and then the capturing of fortifications. Catapults were also much used in training, as in combat, and twenty-mile marches were regularly made with full armor and equipment. A phrase was used that combat was no different from training except for blood.

Good health was essential and was ensured by regular baths and good food. Each legionary base had its baths, and regular bathing in properly heated Roman baths continued through these centuries. With the fall of Rome, regular bathing went out in western Europe, not to be resumed for fourteen hundred years.

Although in the second and third centuries meat and wine were part of the soldiers' diet, in the first century, it was made up primarily of soup, bread, vegetables, lard, and vinegar mixed with water. One is reminded that Christ on the cross said, ''I thirst,'' and was given vinegar on a sponge.[3] This was doubtless sour wine vinegar and water given from the rations of the Roman soldiers guarding the crucifixion area. That it

Hadrian's Wall, built by legionnaires in 122-124, ran 70 miles near the present Scottish border and marked the northern frontier of the Roman Empire. Constructed largely of stone, it was 20 feet high and 8 feet thick.

was a gesture of compassion from a soldier to one he then admired is made more than plausible by the statement of the centurion in command at the moment of Christ's death: "Truly this man was the Son of God."[4]

That the soldiers' diet was a good one[5] is exemplified by the fact that during those three centuries, the average height of the soldier increased several inches. Also, the life expectancy of the retired soldier seems to have been excellent. Julius Valens, a veteran of II Augusta, died at Caerleon near Cardiff at the age of 100, his wife at 75. T. Flavius Virilis, a retired centurion from Britain, died at 70 in Algeria, having served in all three of the legions stationed in Britain as well as III Parthica and III Augusta.[6]

One of the most important qualities of the legion was its many capabilities. Every soldier was also an engineer, and the legion built roads, walls, bridges, theaters, and ships. They mined silver and gold, dug canals, and manufactured not only weapons but also pottery, shoes, and other needed items. These works were not on a small scale. Hadrian's Wall, which ran the seventy miles from Newcastle to Carlisle, was constructed largely of stone. It was built by XX Valeria Victrix, VI Victrix, and II Augusta over the three-year period of 122-124. Twenty years later, the same three legions built the thirty-nine-mile Antonine Wall farther north. Much of Hadrian's Wall still stands today.

One strategically valuable legionary work was the canal dug in 58, connecting the Saone and the Moselle rivers in France. Troop movements to Germany could now be made by water via the Zuider Zee.

In the first century, III Augusta built the road from Thevesta (Tebessa) in Algeria to Carthage in Tunisia, about 180 miles. This legion saw almost all of its service in North Africa, where it is first identified A.D. 6. It was disbanded 232 years later by Gordian III for failing to support him in his bid to become emperor. We are fortunate to have preserved some of Emperor Hadrian's words when he addressed the centurions of the legion and auxiliary troops during an inspection in 128 at Lambaesis. Needless to say, they are words of praise.[7]

One important aspect of the legions was their uniformity. A centurion from a legion in Spain transferred to one in Arabia would find on arrival an encampment identical to the one he had just left. It was laid out in a square, surrounded by a ditch and four walls, each with its gates and streets that ran to the center of the camp. There, in the center, was housed, or rather enshrined, the eagle of the legion. This standard was its totem, the symbol of its life, its history, and its greatness. Directly below the standard was the bank. All soldiers were required to bank part of their pay, to be returned to them when they retired or transferred. Similarly separate money chests were also maintained there for each cohort where was deposited one-half of the cash gifts made on various occasions by the emperors to the soldiers. The members of the legion made certain that their bank never fell into enemy hands. Next to the bank was the commander's house. He alone could have his wife and family with him. Here, in the central area, in their designated locations, were the storehouses, the infirmary, and the armory. Around them, in regular formation, were the troop barracks, each separate room housing eight men and ten such rooms making up a century. The centurion usually had an eleventh room to himself. There was no general mess, but each eight-man squad prepared its own meals at an established hour, using the rations issued to it, supplemented by squad purchases. The centurions ran a tight schedule with no wasted time or motion.

Discipline was strict within the legion, and the centurions had almost complete control. Whole cohorts, however, might be punished. The most violent punishment, rarely used, was *decimation*. In the year 21, a regular cohort in Algeria broke and ran from tribal raiders. The cohort was decimated; selected by lot, every tenth man was flogged to death. In the year 68 or 69, I Adiutrix, a relatively new legion made up of former sailors from the Roman navy, was ordered decimated by the emperor Galba when it refused to respect his authority as emperor.

During the three centuries when the legions were supreme, a number of changes took place that were necessary to conform with the changing conditions. None of them, however, altered the basic quality of the legion. Early in the period, the first cohort of each legion was increased to include five double centuries of 160 men each for a total strength of 800 men. The other nine cohorts remained at six centuries each or 480 men. To the ten cohorts was added a cavalry detachment of 120 horsemen, giving a total strength for the legion of 5,240.

Another important change was an increase of the years of service from twenty to twenty-four. By Hadrian's time, 117-138, this had crept up to twenty-five or twenty-six years, a change that did not go well with the troops. The number of legions also varied but gradually increased. In 37, the original twenty-eight had been reduced to twenty-five, but during Vespasian's rule there were thirty-one. In Trajan's time, 98-117, it was back to thirty. In 161, it was thirty-three, and in 165, again thirty. During Caracalla's time, 211-217, the number was again thirty-three. The variation in number resulted from the abolition of some legions for opposing an emperor and the creation by emperors of legions designed to be particularly faithful to them. One example is VII Galbiana, raised in Spain in 68, and brought to Rome by the new and short-lived emperor Galba. It was then sent off to the Danube area and disbanded a few years later by the emperor Vespasian. Despite these variations of the original twenty-eight Augustan legions, fifteen were apparently still going strong in the fourth century.

After the revolt of 89, Emperor Domitian made two important changes. He forbade the stationing of two legions at the same camp, and he limited the amount of money that could be held in the legion bank. Gallienus, 260-268, forbade senators of Rome from commanding legions or even serving with the army. These last steps were taken to prevent the legions from becoming a base for replacing the emperor of the moment. There was good reason for this thinking. Following the death of Nero in June 68, Galba became emperor. He was killed in January 69, and Otho wore the purple until the legions loyal to him were overcome, resulting in his suicide. Vitellius then took over in Rome, to be killed himself in December 69 after his forces lost the second battle of Cremona to legions loyal to the next emperor, Vespasian.

The second battle of Cremona, described in inaccurate and confusing detail by Tacitus,[8] was a near disaster for the empire, for it drew legions from all the frontiers, opening these lands to foreign invasion. In a night engagement, six legions supporting Vespasian, with the help of auxiliary cavalry, overcame six legions belonging to the Vitellian cause. The latter were helped, unsuccessfully, by elements of three more legions brought over from Britain: II Augusta, XII Gemina, and XX Valeria Victrix. It is interesting to note that after the succession was settled, all the legions, not much the worse for wear, returned to their stations and continued their missions of defending the frontiers.

The British legions were unsuccessful not only at Cremona but also in two other efforts to establish their own chosen emperor. In 196, Albinus, a pretender to the purple, took II Augusta, VI Victrix, and XX Valeria Victrix to Gaul; his forces were defeated at Lyon, where Albinus lost his life. A century later, in 289, these legions gave Carausius, still another aspirant for the role of emperor, a victory in Gaul. Yet after he had acquired northeast France, he was assassinated by his first minister, Allectus. Constantinus, in 296, brought Britain back under Diocletian's control.

The great period of the legions came to an end during the time of Diocletian, 284-305, who increased the number of legions to sixty while diminishing their effectiveness and eliminating the close support of cavalry to infantry. The volunteer quality of the army then diminished, and its increased size required the drafting of soldiers.

It should not be assumed that the legions did all the fighting or that they were, without exception, successful in combat. There were throughout this period as many men serving in the auxiliary formations as there were in the legions, about one hundred and fifty thousand in each category, for a total armed force of three hundred thousand. The auxiliary troops were normally organized in five-hundred-man cohorts under Roman commanders. The troops usually were not Roman citizens, and they drew only half the pay of their opposite numbers in the legions. There was a large amount of auxiliary cavalry with a few formations as large as a thousand horsemen. It must be remembered, however, that the stirrup had not yet been invented; as a result, the horseman, without seated leverage, did not have the combat capability that developed in the Middle Ages when the stirrup came from Asia to western Europe. Some auxiliary units were made up of tribal soldiers under their own chiefs, but these were rare and a late development. Most soldiers were from Roman provinces such as Spain, Gaul, Egypt, or Britain. During most of the period, recruiting was not a problem. Like the legion soldier, the auxiliary trooper, on retirement, received a bounty from the emperor and, what was more important, Roman citizenship. A bronze plaque was posted in Rome naming him as a citizen and a bronze copy sent to him in his place of retirement.

These auxiliary units manned the actual frontier outposts and put out the brush fires. The legions, backing them up, were only rarely called on and then only when there was a major invasion. Some auxiliary cohorts remained in place, successfully doing their jobs literally for centuries. Cohort IV Gallorum was at Chesterholm, a fort on Hadrian's Wall, in 213 and was still there in 410. It is reported that Cohort IX Batavorum had been at Passau for almost four hundred years when, in the middle of the fifth century, the pay chest failed to arrive. Some soldiers who were sent to Rome to get the pay were killed on the way. Thus did Cohort IX Batavorum learn that Rome had fallen.

As to the legions always being successful, there were occasional exceptions. One unfortunate legion was XII Fulminata, which participated in the effort to take Jerusalem in November 66 and was chased almost all the way back to the coast by the Jewish forces. When Jerusalem was finally captured and destroyed in 70, five legions, with auxiliary units attached, were required to do the job. The shame, however, of XII Fulminata was not wiped out, and the legion was banished from Syria and stationed at Melitene on the Euphrates. One of the original Augustan legions, it was to distinguish itself later when, in 172, Marcus Aurelius led it over the Danube to break the power of the Quadi and again in 232 when the emperor Alexander Severus used it in the invasion of Persia. At the very beginning of the period, three legions, XVII, XVIII, and XIX, were wiped out in Saxony, but five years later the Romans reconquered the area. These legion numbers were never used again. Although the legions did not win every battle, they won almost every campaign. For three hundred years, some thirty legions, about 150,000 men, supported by 150,000 auxiliaries, maintained internal security and defended the 4,000 miles of frontier of an empire of 70 million people. This empire included England and Wales, all of western Europe to the Rhine, Austria, Hungary, Rumania, Bulgaria, Yugoslavia, Albania, Greece, Turkey, Syria, Lebanon, Israel, Egypt, Libya, Tunisia, Algeria, Morocco, and parts of Armenia, Persia, and Saudi Arabia.

Five

The Legions in Roman Britain

Six legions participated in the conquest, occupation, and defense of Britain. Of the four that were used by the emperor Claudius for the invasion of the island in 43, two, II Augusta and XX Valeria Victrix, were to remain stationed in Britain for almost four hundred years. The third of the invading legions, XIV Gemina, was moved to the Rhineland in 70, and the fourth, IX Hispana, had been withdrawn to Nijmegen, Holland, prior to 120. II Adiutrix came to Britain in 70 and was sent from there to the Danube eighteen years later. VI Victrix was brought to Britain by the emperor Hadrian in 120 when he was establishing the northern frontier and beginning the construction of Hadrian's Wall. It was to remain stationed in Britain for almost three centuries.

This chapter tells the stories of three of the legions mentioned above, but some discussion of the continuing impact of the legions after the decline of Rome seems appropriate. In 410, the emperor Honorius wrote to the British that they must, in the future, look to their own resources for defense against German and Scandinavian raiders. By this time, the effective troops of the legions had undoubtedly been withdrawn, but the concepts of training and discipline remained. They carried over to the troops organized by the British rulers, and no doubt the retired legionnaires helped in the maintenance of these concepts. Three British rulers were able, thus, to preserve at least a part of Roman Britain for another two hundred years.

The first of these rulers, Vortigern, claimed to be the grandson of the emperor Magnus Maximus. He brought German troops to Britain to help defend the country. These German troops revolted, and Vortigern spent years fighting against them. The second ruler was Ambrosius Aurelanis. According to the various interpretations of the very scarce records of these times, he came to power about 460, claimed imperial ancestry, and successfully fought off the Irish, the Picts, the Scots, and the Saxons.

There are very faint historical records of the last of the three, Artorius, whose family owned one of the great estates. About 475, he took over command of the British forces and was so successful in holding back the various enemies that some historians credit him with fifty years of peace and prosperity, and at least one historian names him as the last Roman Emperor of the West. His greatest battle, about 495, at an unlocated spot called Mons Badon, brought about the defeat of a large Saxon army by a small British one. He is the historical figure on whom the legendary King Arthur is based.

Artorius was killed in battle about 515, and then, slowly, Roman Britain began to unravel. The cities, already in trouble because of the collapse of trade, fell one by one to the invaders. In 552, Salisbury fell; in 571, it was the turn of Gloucester, Cirencester, and Bath. By 600, London was gone, and British rule survived only in Wales and in one or two small kingdoms north of the wall that the Romans had sponsored as buffer states. One of these, Strathclyde, survived all invasions and, in 1018, was absorbed into the Scottish crown. Its capital, the Rock of Dumbarton (Dumbarton means in Celtic the fort of the British), finds its name transported by Scottish immigrants to the capital of the United States and to the famous Harvard study center there, Dumbarton Oaks.

VI VICTRIX

Caracalla

VI Victrix may have been organized by Octavian in the second decade B.C., but is first firmly identified A.D. 9 in Spain. It was last reported in the *Notitia Dignitatis,* the official Roman Army list, 401 years later in York, England.

83

In both 23 and 63, VI Victrix was one of the legions noted in Spain and was, in the latter years, the only legion in Spain. It was in 68 that Sulpicius Galba was proclaimed emperor in the legion's Spanish camp. Galba was an unusual emperor, for, as Plutarch remarks, the job sought him, not he the job. Galba was the wealthiest Roman citizen and was serving as governor of Spain at the time. He had had a distinguished military and governmental career but had reached the age of seventy-three.

Deserted on all sides, Nero committed suicide on 9 June in Rome, his position having become impossible. Galba, still in Spain, was chosen by the senate to be the next emperor. Before starting for Rome late in the summer, he recruited another Spanish legion, VII Galbiana, which accompanied him to Rome. He would have been wiser to have taken VI Victrix with him as well. When he got to Rome, he sent VII Galbiana on to Carnuntum on the Danube east of Vienna. He thus had no troops loyal to him personally. When his old-fashioned virtues of thrift and discipline came to light in a Rome already corrupted by the years of Nero's reign, he became very unpopular. On 15 January 69, Galba was assassinated by troops from the praetorian barracks at the instigation of Otho, who then became emperor. According to Plutarch, only one man fought to protect Emperor Galba. Before the rush of the revolting soldiers, Galba's chair-carriers and guards all fled.[1] A centurion, Sempronius Densus, first tried to turn back the rebels with his vine switch, the symbol of authority. This failing, he drew his sword and engaged them all until he was brought down by a cut under the knees. One would like to think that this man was a centurion of either VI Victrix or VII Galbiana. More likely he was a praetorian loyal to the emperor.

The following year, Vespasian, who had become emperor after the very brief reigns of Otho and Vitellius, sent VI Victrix from Spain to Germany as part of the eight-legion force concentrated to put down the revolt of Civilis. In the year 80, the legion is identified at Novaesium (Neuss), on the Rhine thirty miles north of Cologne. In 89, Antonius Saturninus, Roman governor of upper Germany, led a revolt against the emperor

Domitian. The legions of lower Germany remained loyal, and VI Victrix, which had been moved to Vetera near Xanten, six miles north of Cologne, participated in the defeat of the rebel forces. As a reward for this decisive action, it was honored with the new and additional title of *Pia Fidelis Domitiano,* as were three other legions, I Minervia, X Gemina, and XXII Primigenia.

About 120, then emperor Hadrian brought the legion from Vetera over to Britain. It was stationed at Newcastle, but its headquarters is shown very shortly thereafter at York. There had been uprisings in Britain, and Hadrian had determined to construct a wall from Newcastle to Carlisle to control this area. The wall was built by this legion and two others, XX Valeria Victrix and II Augusta. VI Victrix built the east end of the wall and, in addition, constructed a temple at Newcastle to the Roman gods Neptune and Ocean.

When completed, Hadrian's Wall served not as a fortification but more as a sentry walk. Manned by auxiliary troops, the wall was a base from which cohorts could move out and engage enemies to the north. Another wall, farther north, the Antonine, was built by the same three legions twenty years later, but it did not prove successful and was largely abandoned twenty years after its construction.

Widespread revolt appears to have taken place in 155-158, requiring heavy fighting by the legion. Reinforcements were brought from Germany in 158 as fillers for the three legions that had been seriously reduced in strength by the fighting.

In 196, Albinus, governor of Britain, took VI Victrix, together with the other two legions, to the continent in an effort to establish himself as emperor. After his defeat, the legions returned to Britain to find York and Hadrian's Wall completely overrun. York was recaptured and had to be rebuilt by VI Victrix. The wall was restored by 205, and in 208 the emperor Severus came to Britain to lead personally a punitive expedition against invaders from the north. Troops of the legion were used by the emperor in his northern expeditions, which continued until 211 when the emperor died at York. Severus was succeeded by Caracalla, who had accompanied him to Britain. Caracalla conducted still another expedition, which was highly successful. From this time on, until almost the end of the third century, Britain was relatively peaceful.

The next real break in the peace came in 287, when Carausius set himself up as emperor of Gaul and Britain. He was murdered by Allectus, who, in turn, was defeated in 293, when Constantius Chlorus invaded from the continent and brought Britain back into the empire. In this war, the northern frontier again was stripped of troops and again overrun from the north. Again, VI Victrix returned and had to rebuild its base at York and portions of the wall.

For the next seventy years, conditions were stable, and Britain was prosperous. But in 367, a combined assault by Scots, Picts, and Saxons once more overthrew the wall. After the emperor Valentinian sent Theodosius with an adequate force to suppress the uprising, York and the wall had to be restored once more. Again, Britain was prosperous and relatively peaceful despite disasters in other parts of the empire. Barbarians were, however, knocking at the gates of the continental provinces. The emperor Honorius withdrew most of the combat troops from Britain in 403, including XX Valeria Victrix, leaving a shadowy VI Victrix still at York when Roman rule over Britain came to an end in 410. In that year, Honorius wrote to remaining authorities in Britain that they were entirely on their own and could look for no more help from Rome.

XX VALERIA VICTRIX

Magnus Maximus

Records for Valeria Victrix, one of the original Augustan legions, also cover over four hundred years.

The first firm date is A.D. 6, when it was part of Tiberius's army in Illyricum (Yugoslavia). It derives its name from a commander in the Illyricum wars, Valerius Messalinus.

By 13, the legion had been moved to the Rhine frontier and in 37 was stationed at Novaesium (Neuss), fifty miles north of Cologne. In 43, the emperor Claudius used it, with two other legions, for the invasion and conquest of Britain.

In 61, Valeria Victrix was the main element that finally crushed the British uprising led by Boudicca.[2] Earlier, her forces had badly mauled IX Hispana at Camulodunum, causing some two thousand casualties. The victory of the Roman forces was made more difficult by the failure of II Augusta to follow orders and intervene at the critical moment. Its acting commander, the camp prefect, Poenius Postumas, killed himself when he found out how costly his failure to respond had been. XX Valeria was given the additional title of "Victrix" for its part in the campaign.

At least part of the legion participated, on the losing side, in the second battle of Cremona, forty miles southeast of Milan. Vitellius had been hailed emperor by the legions on the Rhine and had moved on to Rome. Vespasian had been proclaimed emperor in Alexandria and elsewhere. His forces were moving on Rome when this decisive battle was fought at night with some fifteen legions involved. With Vespasian's victory, the troops of XX Valeria Victrix were returned to Britain with the legion stationed first at Gloucester, then at Wroxster and then more permanently at Chester on the northern border of Wales. Under the command of Julius Agricola, a future governor of Britain, the legion helped suppress another British uprising in 69 and 70.

Eight years later, when Julius Agricola became governor, he used his old legion in the conquest of northern Wales and the destruction of the rebellious Ordovices. In 84, the legion was probably the main element in the victory over the Caledonian tribes at Mons Graupius. That victory put the Romans in control of lowland Scotland.[3]

In 122 or 123, the legion joined II Augusta and VI Victrix in starting the construction of Hadrian's Wall between Carlisle and Newcastle. This tremendous military work was not completed until 128, but today it remains the largest structure surviving from the Roman world. Twenty years later, the same three legions built the shorter but less successful Antonine Wall farther north.

As was mentioned earlier, Albinus, governor of Britain in 196, took all three legions from Britain to Gaul to support his effort to become emperor. A decisive battle took place near Lyon with the forces of Severus, who had legions from the Danube and Rhine frontiers. Albinus lost both the battle and his life, and the three legions from Britain were returned, apparently little depleted, to their former stations. The emperor Severus, with the hope of preventing similar events in the future, divided Britain into two provinces so that no governor could command three legions. The legion was at Chester in both 208 and 220.

XX Valeria Victrix appears to have made another incursion on the continent when the usurper Magnus Maximus, with an army from Britain in 383, took over Gaul and Spain in addition to Britain. The emperor Gracian was in Paris and fled to Lyon, where Maximus's cavalry caught up with him and executed him. Maximus, who had received a reluctant acknowledgment by Theodosius, overextended himself by trying to take over Italy and other parts of the empire. He got as far as Milan but had to turn west to meet Theodosius's army coming up from the Danube area. At Siscia, in Yugoslavia, southeast of Zagreb, Maximus's forces were defeated, and he tried to escape to Italy. He was caught and executed at Aquileia just west of Trieste. Once more, the legion found itself returned to Chester.

About 403, XX Valeria Victrix made its final departure from Britain. The emperor Honorius was being besieged by Alaric at Astra near Turin, and his general, Stilicho, rounded up all available troops, including this legion. He arrived in time to save the emperor and soundly defeat Alaric on Easter Sunday at Pollentia, twenty-five miles southeast of Turin.

IX HISPANA

Drusus

Unlike XX Valeria Victrix and VI Victrix, the record of IX Hispana is relatively brief and covers only 155 years. There are vague interpretations that may refer to it as early as 43 B.C., but the first clear reference is A.D. 6 when it was transferred from Spain, where it had obviously been long stationed, to Hungary. Three years later, it is shown at Siscia in northeast Yugoslavia southeast of Zagreb.

In 14, after the death of the emperor Augustus and the

accession of Tiberius, the legion, which was in summer camp with VIII Augusta and XV Apollinaris in western Yugoslavia, joined the other two in a mutiny. Nearby villages were looted as well as the town of Nauportus, present-day Vrhnika, forty miles north of Fiume. The troops demanded shorter terms of service, claiming that some soldiers were being held in the ranks for thirty years. More pay was also demanded. IX Hispana played a moderating role when the men of the other two legions almost came to blows as to whether a certain centurion should be executed. Other centurions found hiding places, according to the detailed description by Tacitus,[4] except for one named Lucilius, who was killed by his men. He had been nicknamed ''Another Please''for his habit of breaking his staff on a soldier's back and then shouting for another and still another.

To the rebel legions, Tiberius sent his son Drusus, who, despite many promises, was failing to make much headway until there occurred what seems to have been, from Tacitus's account, an eclipse of the moon. The troops thought this an ill omen, and then a violent storm convinced them that they were in trouble. Drusus took advantage of this opportunity and had the ringleaders killed. Early winter storms then developed, and these helped bring the troops into line. All three legions marched off to their more comfortable permanent winter quarters. Thus ended the mutiny.

Guerrilla warfare having broken out in the province of Africa (Tunisia), IX Hispana, apparently then in good shape, was dispatched in the year 20 to help restore order. It seems to have been fairly successful, for in 24 it was returned to its old headquarters at Siscia, leaving III Augusta to hold the Tunisian frontier. Nineteen years later, it was used in the invasion of Britain where it was to stay for the remainder of the century.

In 43, with II Augusta, XIV Gemina, and XX Valeria Victrix, IX Hispana landed in Kent for the campaign in Britain. By 48, with the legions spreading out over Britain, IX Hispana was established at Lincoln, 130 miles north of London. Its occupation duties were interrupted in 60 by the very serious uprising led by Boudicca, queen of the Iceni. The queen's forces overran and wiped out the small garrison at Colchester fifty miles northeast of London and destroyed the colony of retired soldiers recently established there. IX Hispana hastened to intervene and was badly mauled by the rebels and took extensive casualties. The then governor of Britain, Suetonius Paulinus, had to abandon both London and St. Albans to the queen's forces. He regrouped, however, and the following year decisively defeated the rebels and destroyed their capability for further effort. London and Colchester, having been burned to the ground, were rebuilt. IX Hispana moved from Lincoln to York, where it had settled by 62. It was brought up to strength with two thousand replacements from Germany.

Gnaeus Julius Agricola, a one-time commander of the legion, served as governor of Britain from 78 to 84. He was the father-in-law of the historian Tacitus and got a very good press from him regarding the campaigns in Scotland. In 83, IX Hispana was attacked in its advanced Scottish encampment by a large force of rebels and was relieved only in the nick of time by Agricola's other forces. Needless to say, Tacitus gives a vivid account of the battle, with the soldiers of IX Hispana making a sally from their base when they hear the approach of the relieving forces. The final battle, which brought peace for some years to the area, was fought the following year at Mons Graupius,[5] where the combined highland forces were crushed.

After these campaigns, the legion went back to York, its permanent base, where its presence is noted in 86, 88, and 110.

Among the historians, there was some controversy about the future of the legion. Some believed that it was wiped out by A.D. 119 in a British uprising.[6] This theory is no longer generally accepted, and it is now believed that the legion was brought back from Britain to the continent by the emperor Trajan in the early part of the second century when it was stationed at Nijmegen, Holland. From here it was transferred to the East and probably destroyed in the war with Parthia in 161. After that date, there are no further mentions of IX Hispana. In its 155 years, it had served Rome in Spain, Hungary, Yugoslavia, Tunisia, Britain, Holland, and Armenia.

Six

Jerusalem and Alexandria

The campaign that resulted in the capture and destruction of Jerusalem in 70 is one of the most completely recorded of all Roman conquests, thanks to Josephus, the capable commander of the Jewish defense. Josephus, after his capture, turned quisling and aided the Romans in every way he could. After the fall of Jerusalem, he went to Rome. There he wrote his famous history of the Jewish War, which defends his every action. Josephus's volume also contains the most detailed report that has come down to us on the organization, training, and tactics of the Roman legions.

Five legions were used in the campaign, which started when Nero was emperor and ended when Vespasian wore the purple. Vespasian himself conducted the first part of this war, and when he went off to Rome, his son Titus, who was to succeed his father as emperor, completed it. Of the five legions, three are reported on in this chapter, V Macedonica, XV Apollinaris, and X Fretensis. The last mentioned was commanded during the campaign by M. Ulpius Trajanus, the father of still another future emperor. The other two legions, VI Ferrata and XII Fulminata, are covered in Chapter IV.

Alexandria loomed large in the Roman world, and both V Macedonica and XV Apollinaris saw service there, not all of it pleasant.

V MACEDONICA

The footprints of V Macedonica can be followed for three hundred years in eastern Europe and the Middle East. An Augustan legion, it was probably formed by 25 B.C. It is first

Titus

specifically mentioned in Syria in 15 B.C., having come from Macedonia where it had been stationed the previous year and from whence it drew its name. By A.D. 23, it had been moved north to Bulgaria as part of the army of the Danube. From there, it was sent to Turkey.

V Macedonica had still been at Pontus in 57 and 58 when X Fretensis participated in the capture of the Armenian capital at Artaxata. About the year 63, Nero moved it from Pontus in northern Turkey to Melitene in eastern Turkey, a key crossing of the Euphrates. At Melitene, the Roman general, Corbulo, concentrated four legions, including VI Ferrata, III Gallica, and XV Apollinaris, for the successful Armenian campaign of that year. It was, in reality, more a show of force than a campaign.

In 67, the legion joined with X Fretensis, XV Apollinaris, and auxiliary troops to make up the army that Vespasian used in the opening of the Jewish War. Vespasian first captured Gamara, twenty miles south of Tyre, which he burned to the ground and where he killed the entire adult population. Next came the town of Jotapata, where the historian Josephus commanded the Jewish forces. According to the account of Josephus, the siege was protracted, with the Romans suffering many casualties. Vespasian is reported to have used 160 projectile hurlers as well as a great battering ram to breach the wall. Josephus's troops made many sorties and gave X Fretensis a bad time, invading its very camp in one of its attacks.

Japha, a town near Jotapata, observing the success of the defenders, revolted against the Romans. Vespasian sent M. Ulpius Trajanus, the father of the future emperor Trajan and then commander of X Fretensis, with one thousand horsemen and two thousand infantry to handle the situation. Titus, Vespasian's son, then followed with more horsemen and one cohort of infantry. The town fell after a six-hour assault largely because most of the defenders had been caught outside the walls by Trajan. These Jewish soldiers had been wiped out, unable to get back into Japha or escape the Romans. The males of Japha were killed and the females and children sold into slavery.

To the south, in Samaria, another situation arose with Samarian troops concentrated at Mt. Gerizim. This problem fell on Ceralius, commander of V Macedonica, who handled it with 3,000 infantry and 600 cavalry. Surrounding the enemy force, he offered them terms, guaranteeing their safety if they would throw down their arms. As they refused, Ceralius attacked and wiped out the entire force, which, according to the gross exaggeration of Josephus, numbered 11,600.

Back at Jotapata, the siege continued into July 67, until the forty-seventh day, when the Roman platforms overtopped the wall. A night assault was led by Titus and was entirely successful. The town was destroyed; two days later, Josephus was found hiding with some twenty others in a pit. He finally surrendered and was kindly treated by Titus and Vespasian. V Macedonica was then sent to winter at Caesarea, on the coast forty miles northwest of Jerusalem.

In the next campaign, the legion had a rather bad time at Gamala, just east of the Sea of Galilee. After the Romans had broken in through the walls, they were chased out again. Vespasian was almost captured in the city. The siege was continued. Finally, the enemy was forced into the citadel in October 67. They held out until a great wind storm came up, which helped the Romans by greatly lengthening the trajectory of their spears and arrows while having the opposite effect on the defenders. There were no survivors, and Josephus says that more died by committing suicide than were actually killed by the Romans.

We next find V Macedonica at Emmaus, ten miles west of Jerusalem, holding this approach to the capital while other troops secured the surrounding area. When news arrived of the death of Nero in June 68, Vespasian delayed the attack on Jerusalem itself. He then turned over the campaign to his son Titus, who concentrated the legions, including V Macedonica, at the capital. The siege was a long one, and platforms were built by the legions to overlook the city walls. V Macedonica's tower was undermined by the Jews; it collapsed and had to be entirely rebuilt. Finally, having broken through the first wall, the legion found itself facing a second one, equally strong. At two in the morning, the standard-bearer of the legion, with a trumpeter and twenty men, by stealth got on top of this wall. The sound of the trumpet fooled the defenders, who ran, and then the other Roman troops followed into the city. There was much hard fighting, but the city was finally captured and destroyed in September 70.

After the destruction of Jerusalem, Titus moved with V Macedonica to Caesarea, where the booty was secured. From there, he marched with the legion over the desert to Alexandria. Titus then took a boat to Rome while V Macedonica was dispatched to Bulgaria. The legion was stationed at Oescus on the Danube. It was still there in 96, but by 108 it had been moved to Troesmis, farther down the Danube in Romania. V Macedonica remained there until 167, when it was moved to Potaissa, 150 miles north of the Danube in central Transylvania. In due course, Rome decided not to hold this area north of the Danube, and V Macedonica was returned to Oescus by 274.

In 296, Narses of Persia decided to take Syria from the Romans. Galerius, the Roman commander there, was defeated. The emperor Diocletian gave Galerius something of a tongue lashing and told him to try again; but this time he was given V Macedonica as a key element in his force. Narses was later badly defeated by Galerius's troops. When Ctesiphon fell, the wife and children of Narses of Persia were captured, together with great booty. Mesopotamia was surrendered to Rome, and Persia recognized a Roman protectorate over Armenia.

This campaign can be thought of as the last for V Macedonica as a true legion. Shortly thereafter, Diocletian expanded the army to sixty legions and split V Macedonica into two legions, apparently of the same name but each less than half strength. The newer legion was sent off for service in Egypt.

XV APOLLINARIS

XV Apollinaris was named for Augustus's protecting deity and was probably formed by Augustus when he was still known as Octavian, prior to the battle of Actium in 31 B.C. First stationing of XV Apollinaris is indicated in southern Yugoslavia.

It seems to have been moved prior to A.D. 14 to Emona on the River Save, fifty miles northeast of Trieste. It participated in the revolt of 14. In 37, the legion is reported as having moved again, this time to Carnuntum, now Hamburg, on the Danube. In 63, it was sent to Melitene on the Euphrates

Etruscan Apollo

where, under the command of Corbulo, it joined with three other legions in an impressive Armenian campaign.

After the Armenian campaign, XV Apollinaris helped to put down an insurrection at Alexandria. As a result of an incident in the amphitheater, the Jewish population of the city attacked the Greeks.[1] Finally two legions, including Apollinaris, were ordered by the city governor, Tiberius Alexander, to overrun the Jewish area known as Delta. After a pitched battle, the legions killed thousands of Jews and looted and destroyed their homes. Oddly enough, according to Josephus, the looting and killing stopped at once when Alexander gave the order.

Because of the revolt of the Jews in Galilee, Samaria, and Judea, Titus was dispatched by his father Vespasian to bring the legion from Alexandria to Ptolemais, on the Mediterranean coast twenty miles south of Tyre, where it joined V Macedonica and X Fretensis for the campaign to restore Roman rule.

First Gamara, about twelve miles to the east, together with the adjacent villages, was captured and destroyed. The city of Jotapata was then put under siege, with Josephus commanding the defending forces. The siege took forty-eight days. In the final night assault on the city, Titus led a small group from XV Apollinaris, which achieved complete surprise and ended the defense.

After this victory, the legion, with the other two legions, was sent to refit at Scythopolis, thirty-five miles east of Caesarea. In September, Vespasian concentrated his forces at Scythopolis and moved against Tarichaeae, on the west shore of the Sea of Galilee. Here he found that the defenders, when unable to save the town, took to their boats and continued to fight from them. Vespasian then had his troops build rafts, which he manned with his own forces. The sea battle resulted in complete victory for the Romans, with great loss of life among the Jewish sailors and destruction of most of the Jewish craft.

In October, Gamala, on the other side of the Sea of Galilee, was besieged. As in other sieges, the Romans built towers, the most important one here being that of XV Apollinaris. Using battering rams and heavy stone hurlers, the wall was finally breached and the Romans poured in. The defenders rallied on high ground and drove out the attackers. It was here that Vespasian himself was almost killed or captured. The city was finally taken in October. After Gamala, XV Apollinaris went with Vespasian to join in the attack on Jerusalem. During this prolonged siege, the legion, under the command of Titus Phrygius, built the tower facing the High Priests monument. This tower was destroyed by the defenders and had to be built a second time. It was a giant battering ram with an iron beak that broke the first section of the wall. The legion also helped in the monumental task of building a wall around the city in three days.

The legion was now moved to Caesarea again, where prisoners were sold into slavery and booty made secure. Then, accompanied by Titus, they traveled back over the desert to Egypt.

From Alexandria, the legion was shipped to Carnuntum on the Danube, east of Vienna, from whence it had come seven years earlier. It was still on the Danube in 93, and again in 110. In 115, the emperor Trajan moved XV Apollinaris permanently to the Middle East, stationing it at Satala in northeast Turkey and about a hundred miles from the Black Sea.

When Alexander was emperor, the legion was reported to be in Satala in 232, about 270 years after its formation. It had spent almost half its time in Europe and half in the Middle East.

X FRETENSIS

Fretensis has a dictionary definition of *straits*, and the body of water referred to in this case is the straits of Messina where Octavian (Augustus) won a naval war against Sextus Pompeius. As an emblem on its standard, the legion had the trireme.

Tiberius

Identifications for the legion cover a period of 250 years, the first being in the year 6, when it was serving as garrison troops in northern Syria. In 18, the legion was in winter quarters north of Antioch at Cyrrhus. In that year, the confrontation in its camp took place between Germanicus, commander in the East, and his unwilling subordinate, Piso.[2] Shortly thereafter, Germanicus died, presumably by poisoning. Piso, on returning to Tiberius's Rome, was accused of murder, and, according to several reports, killed himself when he saw how difficult it would be to clear his name.

Records show X Fretensis still at Cyrrhus in 23, but it was brought north for the Armenian campaign of 57-58 and participated in the capture of the Armenian capital of Artaxata. Tacitus says that the three legions used by the Roman commander Corbulo, which included III Gallica and VI Ferrata, could not provide, even with their auxiliaries, enough troops for a garrison. Thus the city was razed, though the inhabitants were spared. Tiridates, the Armenian commander, had fled with his troops to fight another day.

Shortly thereafter, the legion moved to Cilicia in southeast Turkey, but in 63 it was again back in what was then Syria. M. Ulpius Trajanus, future governor of Syria and father of the future emperor Trajan, was in command of X Fretensis when Vespasian organized his troops for the Jewish war at Ptolemais, present-day Akko, thirty miles south of Tyre on the Mediterranean. X Fretensis had been brought there from the Euphrates, and it was to winter twenty-five miles farther south at the port of Caesarea in Samaria. In 67, the legion was used in the capture of Tarichacae and Gamala on the west and east shores of the Sea of Galilee. Vespasian then based the legion at Scythopolis, present-day Bet She'an, west of the Jordan River. In the campaign to capture Jerusalem, which started in 68 and ended in September 70, the legion was positioned for a time on the Mount of Olives. In 72, the legion went on to capture Macaerus, east of the Dead Sea, in what is now Jordan. This is where, some thirty years earlier, the head of John the Baptist had been presented on a platter to Salome after her famous dance.[3] In 73, X Fretensis attacked Masada, on the west bank of the Dead Sea, in present-day Israel, where the last defenders all committed suicide.

Although Jerusalem had been destroyed, the legion was stationed near the site as a garrison. It was still there in 114 and in 120. In 130, the emperor Hadrian ordered the building of a new city where Jerusalem had stood, and the legion certainly must have had a part in the construction. The new city was to be known as Aelia Capitolina, but the Jews revolted and took the new city by storm in 132. After a severe struggle, the city was captured again by the Romans in 135 and again destroyed. The legion seems to have survived these events, for it was still reported in Judea in 138, and in 232 a report shows it still at Jerusalem. The city had been again rebuilt and was still a Roman colony in 637, when the caliph Omar captured it.

Seven

Armenia, Syria, and Persia

The three legions discussed in this chapter played key roles in the Armenian and Persian wars. They crossed and recrossed Syria, but the most dramatic of the campaigns was the drive down the Tigris and Euphrates rivers to the Persian Gulf. In 114, the legions available to the emperor Trajan for this campaign were III Gallica, VI Ferrata, XII Fulminata, II Traiana, XVI Flavia Firma, IV Scythica, and X Fretensis. This chapter tells the stories of the first three of these legions.

III GALLICA

III Gallica is reported to have been organized by Julius Caesar and at that time given the number III. The legion is supposed to have fought as part of Antony's army in the defeat of the Parthians in 36 B.C. and was based in northern Syria in 4 B.C. as III Gallica. It was probably recruited in Gaul, as its name implies.

Elagabalus as Sun God

In 23, another report shows III Gallica in Syria, and in the time of Claudius, 41-54, it was one of the four legions making up the Syrian garrison. In the Armenian campaign of 58, the legion played a key role. Vologes I of Parthia (Persia) had installed his brother Tiridates as king of Armenia, and the Roman general, Cnaeus Domitius Corbulo, was required to bring Armenia back under Roman control. Apparently, like other Syrian troops, III Gallica was in slack condition and had to be toughened up. Corbulo accomplished this with harsh conditions and discipline. With III Gallica and two other legions, VI Ferrata and X Fretensis, he launched a successful campaign, capturing simultaneously three major fortresses, including Volandum north of Mt. Ararat. Tiridates massed his army before his capital of Artaxata, and, during an entire day, the two armies faced each other, with III Gallica on the left of the Roman line. The following night, the Parthian commander thought better of the fight and withdrew, leaving Artaxata to the Romans' mercy, which was in short supply. The city was razed. Corbulo then concentrated his legions on the Euphrates.

Another Roman commander, Lucius Caesennius Paetus, then went to war with the Parthian army in Armenia. Commanding three legions, he took a bad beating and was allowed to escape from a siege only under humiliating conditions. Paetus's troops double-timed to the Euphrates, where they had the protection of Corbulo's legions. Corbulo was then given overall command of the Roman forces and conducted an insignificant campaign. Thus Tiridates was left as ruler of Armenia. He had only to go to Rome to be invested by the emperor.

In 68, III Gallica was ordered to the Danube front in Yugoslavia. It first defeated the invading Rhoxolani. In the spring of 69, the legion fought a very successful action against nine thousand Sarmatian cavalrymen who had overrun auxiliary troops and were pillaging the Hungarian countryside. The Sarmatians were not only overconfident, but laden with loot. The weather was snowy and the ground soft and wet. The horses had bad footing. The Sarmatians, once unhorsed, were unable to fight on equal terms because of their heavy armor and lack of shields and thus were exterminated.[1]

By October, the legion had reached Italy, moving with other Danube army legions to support the cause of Vespasian against Vitellius. On 24 October, the two armies fought an engagement that started in the afternoon and carried through the night. At dawn the men of III Gallica turned to hail the rising sun in the tradition of the East. Their opponents, not knowing the custom, assumed that they were shouting a welcome to reinforcements and fled.[2] The following day, Vitellius's supporters had withdrawn to a fortified encampment near Cremona. This was assaulted by Vespasian's supporters, and it was III Gallica that first broke through the defenses. Vitellius's troops then withdrew within the walls of Cremona. Once the attack on the town had started, the defending legions, thinking better of resistance, surrendered and marched out to the taunts of the victors. Cremona was then sacked and much of the population seized to be sold into slavery. The city, set afire, burned for four days.

Vespasian's legions, under the command of Antonius Primus, pressed on to Rome where Vitellius, awaiting his doom, was murdered by revolting local troops on 20 December. There was some looting and burning by the Vespasian forces in Rome. III Gallica was billeted in Capua, to the southeast. The legion was rather rough on the local population, particularly the leading families.

From Capua, III Gallica was sent back to Syria. The legion was again in action in 114, this time as part of the army that the emperor Trajan used in his successful war against Parthia. It will be recalled that 150 years earlier, III Gallica had engaged the Parthians. This time, Armenia and Mesopotamia were annexed, and the Parthian capital, Ctesiphon, about fifteen miles south of Baghdad, was captured. Trajan had divided his army into two parts, one going by boat down the Tigris and the other by boat down the Euphrates. The entire army then marched overland for the capture of Ctesiphon. In the winter of 115-116, Trajan continued down to the mouth of the Tigris, establishing temporary Roman dominance at the top of the Persian Gulf.

In 120, the legion was back in Syria and remained there during the reign of Antonius Pius, 138-161.

On 16 May 218, at Raphanaea, about ninety miles south of Antioch, Elagabalus was proclaimed emperor in the legion's camp. The son of the deceased Syrian, Varius Marcellus, a Roman senator, Elagabalus was at this time only fourteen years of age. He was a hereditary priest of the god Baal of Emesa, and was said to be the last of the Antonines. He was completely under the thumb of his mother, Julia Soamias Bassiana, who had engineered the coup.[3]

With his troops under the command of his tutor, Elagabalus advanced in forced marches on Antioch, where the emperor Macrinus organized troops to meet him. An engagement was fought twenty-eight miles south of Antioch, resulting in the complete defeat of Macrinus, most of whose troops deserted him. He tried to escape and flee to Rome but was recognized, despite his disguise, and executed.

III Gallica did not remain faithful to Elagabalus but supported enemies of the new emperor. As a result, the legion was disbanded in 218. By 232, however, it had been reactivated at Raphanaea and was moved to Danaba to cover the Palmyra-Damascus road.

VI FERRATA

The "iron legion," VI Ferrata was, in all probability, one of the legions that Antony used at the battle of Philippi in October 42 B.C. It would not, however, have been known as "Ferrata"at that time.

It is also just possible that it was the
Antony   legion referred to in Chinese history,[4] whose men confronted the forces of the Han Empire in Sogdiana in 36 B.C. Sogdiana, now known as the Turkmen S.S.R., lies to the east of the Caspian Sea on the Oxus River in southern Russia. Antony was campaigning in 36 B.C. to the west and south of the Caspian, and it is possible that a legionary detachment was dispatched in a probing action to the east and north. If the Chinese report is true, it would be the only recorded instance when the forces of the emperors of Rome and China met. One speculates that after seeing each other's troops and sizing up the situation, the two commanders each decided that they lacked the supplies to take on a difficult new enemy.

When Augustus was reorganizing the army in 4 B.C., the soldiers of VI Ferrata were serving as garrison troops in northern Syria. They were stationed near Laodici, south of Antioch, A.D. 19, and again A.D. 23. Under the emperor Claudius, 41-54, they continued as garrison troops for Syria.

In 58, VI Ferrata was part of Corbulo's army that defeated

the forces of Tiridates in Armenia and destroyed the capital, Artaxata.

In November 66, the commander of the legion, Priscus, was killed when XII Fulminata was chased back from Jerusalem almost to the coast by the defenders of that city. It may be assumed that a small element of VI Ferrata was present, for it is unlikely that its commander was merely accompanying XII Fulminata. In any event, VI Ferrata participated in the siege and capture of Jerusalem in 70. After the fall of the Jewish capital, the legion was used in 72 in the clean-up operations, in particular the capture of Macaerus and Masada on either side of the Dead Sea. The legion was then moved north to Samsat (Samosata), on the Euphrates, two hundred miles northeast of Antioch, where it may have been joined by the newly formed XVI Flavia Firma.

In 105, Trajan had determined to take control of all of what is now Jordan and of much of Saudi Arabia. The task was assigned to VI Ferrata and some auxiliary troops and was efficiently accomplished. In 108, the legion served as garrison troops at Bostra in northern Jordan. A great Roman road was built between the years 111 and 114 that ran from the Gulf of Acaba to Petra, Amman (Philadelphia), Bostra, and on to Damascus. It may be assumed that the legion played a major part in construction.

The Roman influence was now so great in this part of the world that a Roman fleet was maintained in the Red Sea and emissaries came to Rome from India.

Because of the legion's experience in the East, it is probable that Trajan used it as a key element of his force that in 115 swept down the Tigris and Euphrates rivers to Baghdad, Ctesiphon, and the Persian Gulf.

In 120, the legion was in or near Antioch, about 130 at Samosata with XVI Flavia firma, in 138 back in Judea, and in 200 in Palestine. The last report available is for the year 232 in the reign of Alexander, when it was moved from Caparcotna, in Palestine, to Phoenice (Lebanon). It disappears some time between 235 and 284.

One particular centurion who served with the legion in the

second century deserves mention, for he illustrates the inter-
change of officers between the legions. Petronius Fortunatus,
said to have come from Africa, probably Tunisia, served several
years with I Italica in Romania, where he became a centurion.
He was then transferred to VI Ferrata in Palestine. Then he
went on to serve in eleven other legions as follows: I Minervia
in lower Germany, X Gemina in Yugoslavia, II Augusta in Britain, III Augusta in Algeria, III Gallica in Syria, XXX Ulpia
in lower Germany, VI Victrix in Britain, III Cyrenaica in Jordan, XV Apollinaris in eastern Turkey, II Parthica at Albano
in Italy, and, last, I Adiutrix in Yugoslavia. After some forty-
six years of service, he retired and presumably went back to
his native Tunisia.[5]

XII FULMINATA

XII Fulminata was part of Trajan's
Middle East army when he undertook the
Parthian campaign and moved down to the
mouth of the Tigris. Another of the original
Augustan legions, it may have origins with
Julius Caesar. Some historians state that it
was once part of Antony's army. Fulminata
means "hurler of lightning."

Julius Caesar

In 30 B.C., the legion was based in Africa, probably
Tunisia. It is reported in Syria A.D. 14, and again in 23.

In 62, XII Fulminata was part of the unfortunate force led
by Paetus that suffered a crushing defeat in Armenia. The
following year, the legion was sent back to Syria to refit. Again,
in 66, it was humiliated, for it was used by C. Cestus Gallus
in an abortive effort to capture Jerusalem. Although supported
by auxiliaries and some elements from other legions, it was
chased all the way back to Antipatris, forty miles away. In the
retreat it lost its eagle and all its siege train and other equipment. This unlucky legion partially redeemed itself, however,
in the forthcoming siege, capture, and destruction of Jerusalem
in 70. Titus did not, however, return it to Syria, but instead
sent it to Melitene, two hundred miles northeast of Antioch.
In 114 XII Fulminata was in Cappadocia (in eastern Turkey)

when Trajan undertook his campaign against Armenia and Mesopotamia and his expedition down to the Persian Gulf. We have no records, however, to tell us whether it was part of the western force that went down the Euphrates, or part of the eastern force that descended the Tigris past Baghdad all the way to the Gulf.

In 138, XII Fulminata was again based in southeastern Turkey. But in 172, Marcus Aurelius led a force, including the legion, across the Danube into the lands of the Quadi, a people living in what is now northern Austria and Czechoslovakia. The emperor's base was the legion camp at Carnuntum east of Vienna, near Hainburg. For three years, he relentlessly pursued the Quadi and their allies from this base. It was during this campaign that Marcus Aurelius began writing his famous *Meditations.*

There is a story from this war, often repeated, of a victory for XII Fulminata in Moravia when a miraculous rainstorm put the enemy to flight. The rainstorm was attributed to the prayers of the Christian soldiers of this Cappadocian legion.

By 231, the legion had been moved to Melitene on the Euphrates in eastern Turkey. The last campaign in which reports show XII Fulminata playing a part is the Persian War of 232. The then emperor, Alexander Severus, concentrated his legions in the general area of Antioch where he himself, with his mother, led the forces against the Persian king of kings, Ardashir, who was bent on reestablishing the old Persian Empire.

The campaign was no success for either the Romans or the Persians. The emperor advanced eastward in three columns. Ardashir first brought the northern column to a halt and then turned south and defeated the southern column. The emperor was presumably with the central column which, due to the cautiousness of Severus, never engaged the enemy.

Ardashir must also have suffered serious losses, for he broke off contact and withdrew eastward while the Romans withdrew to the Antioch area. It may be assumed that XII Fulminata was then returned to its base at Melitene.

Eight ───────────────────────────────

More Augustan Legions

When the emperor Augustus died in the year 14, he bequeathed to the Roman Empire an army containing twenty-five legions. Of these, nine have been discussed in the three previous chapters, and the movements of the other sixteen are outlined in numerical order in the following chapters.

The locations of these sixteen legions between the years 30 and 130 illustrate the changing pressures on the empire. An important shift of the legions to the east and south was taking place. In the year 30, there were eight legions on the Rhine, six in the general area of the Danube, and four in Turkey, Syria, and Palestine. One hundred years later, there were only five on the Rhine, but the six on the Danube had increased to ten and the four in the Middle East to eight.

Germanicus

I GERMANICA

First noted as part of the army of Octavian before he assumed the title of Augustus, I Germanica suffered a disastrous defeat in Spain. It was subsequently reconstituted by Tiberius. In 14, it was stationed in Germany in a joint camp with XX Valeria Victrix at Cologne. That year, it participated in a revolt, but the successful personal appeal of Germanicus persuaded the troops to return to their loyalty.[1] Germanicus, who was then in command of the Roman armies in both upper and lower Germany, spent much time with the legion, and it may well be that I Germanica derives its name from this man. Apparently given to revolts, the legion joined the uprising of Civilis in 69. Civilis, a Batavian chief, persuaded the legion to take an oath to support his hoped-for Gallic empire. He posted the legion at Trier, the center for the Treveri tribe. When the army of the emperor Vespasian arrived from Rome the following year, the Treveri went over to him. The legion abandoned Civilis and took the oath to Vespasian. In either 70 or 71, unmollified, Vespasian disbanded I Germanica.

II AUGUSTA

Capricorn as Standard

II Augusta is best known for its work in the construction of Hadrian's Wall. The legion was organized by Augustus, had the capricorn as emblem, and, in the year 10, was based on the Rhine frontier. It moved to Strasbourg in 23. Twenty years later, II Augusta was under the command of the future emperor Vespasian. The emperor Claudius used it and three other legions for the invasion of Britain. Records show the legion was stationed at Gloucester in 62. A year earlier its acting commander had committed suicide when he learned that his failing to obey orders had led to the initial success of the uprising by Boudicca.[2]

In 69, elements of II Augusta were sent to the continent to help defend Vitellius from Vespasian's drive for Rome. These elements were on the losing side at the second battle of Cremona and were promptly returned to the legion in Britain. In 75, the legion was moved to Caerleon, in Wales, where it was to be based for the indefinite future. In 122 and 123, it constructed major parts of Hadrian's Wall between England and Scotland and twenty years later helped with the construction of the short-lived Antonine Wall farther north. In 196, the legion was brought to France by the pretender Albinus. When Albinus was defeated by Severus, the legion was returned to Caerleon. In 383, II Augusta made one more trip to France when Magnus Maximus made his unsuccessful effort to take over the empire. After the defeat of Maximus at Milan, the victorious emperor Theodosius once again returned II Augusta to Caerleon. It was probably still in Britain at the beginning of the fifth century, though much diminished in effectiveness.

Hadrian

III AUGUSTA

III Augusta was not a world traveler. Its origin is uncertain, but it was probably formed and given its number by Octavian and given its name by him when he became Augustus. It is first reported in the year 6 at Ammaedara, northeast of Tebessa in Algeria. From there it built the famous military road to Carthage. Reports for 23 and 70 show III Augusta still in Africa, presumably at Ammaedara. About the year 100, the legion helped construct the city of Thamugadi, 100 miles to the west. This was undertaken at the direction of the emperor Trajan. In 120, the legion is reported some twelve miles farther west at Lambaesis, near Batna, south of Algiers. It was here that the emperor Hadrian inspected and addressed the troops in 128.[3]

III Augusta supported Severus in his drive to become emperor, and, as a result, it received the additional title of *Piae Vindicis* in 194. Severus even visited its camp at Lambaesis in 203. In 216, the legion was used by the emperor Caracalla in his Parthian campaign in Mesopotamia.

In 238, back at Lambaesis, III Augusta supported the then emperor, Maximinus, against the rise of the Gordians. In that year, its troops killed Gordian II in battle. As a result, Gordian I killed himself. Gordian III, when firmly established as emperor, understandably disbanded the legion. It was, however, reconstituted at Lambaesis in 253.

Aurelian

III CYRENAICA

The origin of III Cyrenaica is obscure. A part of Augustus's original army organization, this legion must have either come from, or at an early time served in, Cyrenaica in eastern Libya. The first firm report shows the legion in Egypt, either at Thebes or at Coptos, north of Luxor on the Nile. In 119, III Cyrenaica was in the same camp as XXII Deioteriana at

Nicopolis, Egypt. It was sent, probably in 120, to Arabia and stationed at Bostra in northern Jordan, near present-day Irbid. In 216, the legion participated in Caracalla's Parthian campaign in Mesopotamia but was back again in Bostra in 232.

It is likely that the legion was part of the force used by the emperor Aurelian in the defeat of Zenobia and the capture of Palmyra in 272. The beautiful and forceful Zenobia, queen of Palmyra, had gained control of much of Asia Minor, including Syria and Egypt. She styled herself as Queen of the East. Aurelian, determined to restore the unity of the empire, engaged her army first at Antioch and again at Emesa, winning both engagements. Zenobia fell back on Palmyra, but later she attempted to escape the siege of her capital. She was captured on the bank of the Euphrates and taken to Rome to be displayed in the triumph of Aurelian.

The last report we have of III Cyrenaica concerns its looting the temple of the sun god in captured Palmyra.

IV MACEDONICA

Caesar may have formed IV Macedonica, but certainly it was part of Octavian's army when he became Augustus. It was probably stationed in Macedonia at an early date. This legion had a short and not particularly distinguished career. First based in

Galba

Spain in the year 9 and again in 23, it was brought to the Rhineland by Claudius after 39 to replace a legion that had been used in the invasion of Britain. It is reported sharing a double camp at Mainz with XX Primigenia in 43 and again in 69. It participated in the revolt against Galba, failed to support Vespasian, and, as a result, was disbanded by the latter in 70. At this time, Vespasian created two new legions, one of them being IV Flavia Firma, which might have received some of the better veterans from the defunct IV Macedonica.

IV SCYTHICA

The first specific location for IV Scythica was Moesia

Septimus Severus

(Bulgaria) in 23. In 57, this legion went to Syria and later that year to Armenia. In the Armenian campaign of 62 with XII Fulminata, it suffered serious defeat as part of the command of Lucius Caesennius Paetus, and in 63 was sent to Syria to refit. Nero appears to have moved it by 69 to the Euphrates, possibly Zeugma, in present-day southern Turkey. In 72, IV Scythica was either at Cyrrhus or Zeugma. It was reported near Antioch in 120. In 187, Septimus Severus was its commander. He was to become emperor in 193. The legion was in Mesopotamia in 216 as part of the force used by Caracalla in his Parthian campaign. Reported in Syria in 218, it was back in Zeugma by 232.

V ALAUDAE

Julius Caesar

First noted about 50 B.C., V Alaudae is reputed to have been raised by Caesar in Gaul. Its name is the Celtic word for lark, the great singer. It was stationed at Cologne A.D. 17 and in lower Germany A.D. 23. In 29, the legion was mauled by the Frisians and, after the year 40, was stationed at Vetera, known today as Xanten on the lower Rhine. The year 69 was a bad one for V Alaudae. The main body was off on the losing side at the first battle of Cremona. The element left behind at the headquarters at Xanten was wiped out by Civilis during his abortive attempt to establish his Gallic empire. In 87, the legion was stationed on the Danube; in 92, the emperor Domitian launched it over the Danube into what is now Czechoslovakia in a campaign against the Sarmatians, who were raiding Roman lands. In this ill-reported campaign, V Alaudae was completely destroyed, and it appeared no more on Roman army lists.

VII CLAUDIA

VII Claudia at first had the unofficial name of ''Mace-

Caligula

donica'', presumably because at an early time it garrisoned Macedonia. The legion received its formal title and the honorific *pia fidelis* (patriotic and faithful) from the emperor Claudius because of its loyalty when the troops in Dalmatia were urged to revolt A.D. 42 by the governor, Furius Camillus Scribonianus. The legion had first been reported in this part of Yugoslavia in 39, during the reign of Caligula. In 57 or 58, it was moved up to the Danube. Like other legions on the Danube, VII Claudia was drawn into the struggle in 69 between the forces of Vitellius and those of Vespasian. Fortunately, it was on the winning side of the battle of Cremona, reportedly holding the left of the line in the first part of the battle. Afterward, the legion was posted to a new location at Viminacium, near Kostolacz, about forty miles down the Danube from Belgrade, Yugoslavia. Reports show it remained there in 86, 93, and 108. In 115, part of it was used in Trajan's Armenian campaign, but by 120 it had returned again to Viminacium. In 202, it was still there, and in 337, it had an element in upper Moesia, probably at Viminacium.

VIII AUGUSTA

Bearing the name of the emperor, VIII Augusta was established by Augustus and was first reported A.D. 23 at Poetovio, near Marburg, on the Drava River in Yugoslavia. It took part in the short-lived rebellion in 14. About 43, the legion was moved to the Danube area of Moesia, probably Bulgaria.

Gallienus

In 69, it went with the other two Moesian legions to Italy to support the cause of Vespasian at the battle of Cremona. Next, in 70, it was sent to the upper Rhine and stationed at Strasbourg. Reports show VIII Augusta continuing in the upper Rhine area in 83, 90, 110, 120 and 138. In 200, it was reported in lower Germany. The last report, in 258-259, showed VIII Augusta, with the emperor Gallienus, crushing a German invasion of Italy at a major battle at Milan.

X GEMINA

Probus

As its name implies, X Gemina was made up of two other legions. It was first reported in Spain A.D. 9. Another report shows it in Spain in 23. In 63 it was in Pannonia, probably Hungary. The legion returned to Spain in 69, but in 70 it was brought to Germany to help suppress the Civilis uprising. It arrived too late for the battle of Vetera, and it was then established on the lower Rhine near Nijmegen.

During the time of the emperor Domitian, 81-96, X Gemina helped in the suppression of another revolt and was awarded the title *pia fidelis Domitiana.* About 108, the legion moved from Nijmegen to Vienna, where it remained in 193. In 196, it won another honorary title, *pia fidelis Severiana,* for having supported the claim of the new emperor Severus. A report for the year 200 had it still in Vienna. The last report, for the year 260, showed X Gemina in upper Pannonia, presumably in Vienna.

According to the *Augustan History,* the legion could claim as former commanders two emperors, Aurelian and Probus.

Diocletian

XI CLAUDIA pia fidelis

In pre-Augustan days, XI Claudia was sometimes called Actiacus, which might imply that this legion fought in the battle of Actium. It received its formal title A.D. 42 for remaining loyal to the emperor Claudius when a revolt had broken out under the leadership of Furius Camillus Scribonianus. Like VII Claudia, the legion received the honorific title of *pia fidelis.* It was first noted in Dalmatia, A.D. 9, at Burnum, near present-day Knin, in Yugoslavia. It was reported there in 14 and 39. In 70, XI Claudia moved to Switzerland and was stationed at Vindonissa, present-day Windisch, twenty miles east of Basel. After 101, but before 106, it was moved to Silistra (Durostorum), on the Danube in Bulgaria. Here it was reported in 110, 120, 138, and again in 200.

The last known location of the legion was Aquileia in northeast Italy near Monfalcone. From here, Diocletian dispatched a major element for the campaign in North Africa in 288. This element participated in the resecuring of this part of the empire in a drive from Tangier to Carthage.

XIII GEMINA

Vitellius

A composite legion assembled by Augustus, XIII Gemina was reported, A.D. 9, on the Rhine at Windisch in Switzerland. It continued on the Rhine in this area in 14 and 23. In 45 or 46, the legion was sent to Poetovio, present-day Ptuj, near Marburg in Yugoslavia. In 69, the legion had been to Italy and fought on the Vitellian side in the first battle of Cremona and on the Vespasian side in the second. By 96, it had moved to Vienna. Trajan used the legion in his Dacian War of 106, after which it was stationed at Apulum, near present-day Alba Iulia, in Romania. It was again reported there in 120. In 261, XIII Gemina was reported at Mehadia, near present-day Balta, in south-central Romania. Seven years later, it was back again at Poetovio in Yugoslavia. In 274, it was reported at Ratiaria on the Danube in Bulgaria. After 300, the legion was reportedly split permanently into four elements, all stationed at different places on the Danube. It then ceased to function as a legion.

XIV GEMINA

Otho

XIV Gemina, another of Augustus's composite legions, first appeared historically in 9, having been badly beaten in the Varian[4] disaster and reaching safety at Vetera, on the lower Rhine. In 14, the legion was based in Germany, at Mainz. In 43, Claudius used it in the invasion and conquest of Britain, and it was one of the legions that finally crushed the uprising led by Boudicca in 60. For its part in this campaign, XIV Gemina was awarded the additional title of *Martia Victrix*. In

69, major elements of the legion were drawn to Italy to support Otho at the first battle of Cremona and were sent back to Britain by the winner, Vitellius. The following year, the legion was brought back to the continent by the next emperor, Vespasian, to help put down the uprising of Civilis at Xanten. Vespasian stationed it at Mainz. In 89, XIV Gemina was on the wrong side of a revolt against Domitian but was permitted to stay at Mainz for three more years. In 92 it redeemed itself. When XXI Rapax was destroyed on the Danube, Domitian sent for XIV Gemina to restore order. That done, it was then stationed in Pannonia (Hungary) and was noted there in 110. In 236, the legion was still stationed in Pannonia at Carnuntum where, according to the last known report, it remained for at least another 24 years.

XVI GALLICA

Tiberius

XVI Gallica has a brief history; it seems to have had a genius for picking the wrong side. Its name appears to indicate service in Gaul before the first century, and the first recorded location for it was upper Germany A.D. 14. That year, the year of Augustus's death, the legion participated in the short-lived mutiny against Tiberius. By 43, the legion was stationed at Mainz. Before 69, it had been transferred to Novaesium (Neuss), farther down the Rhine near Dusseldorf. The legion made the mistake of siding with Vitellius against the Vespasian forces at the second battle of Cremona. Even worse, the base elements of the legion that had been left behind at Novaesium surrendered to the rebel leader Civilis and were marched in shame from Novaesium to Trier. Shortly thereafter, probably in 70, Vespasian ordered the disbanding of the legion. He then organized a new legion in Asia Minor with the same number but with the name "Flavia firma," Flavia being his family name.

XXI RAPAX

Another legion with a relatively short history, ninety-eight years, is XXI Rapax. It derived its name from *rapax,* meaning rapacious or greedy in the sense of overcoming all. First identified historically in the year 6 in southern Germany, the legion moved to Xanten on the lower Rhine. There it joined the other legions in a short-lived uprising in 14. In 45-46, it was moved to Windisch in Switzerland, near Basel, to re-

Domitian

place XIII Gemina, which had been sent to Poetovio in Yugoslavia. For several years before this move, XXI Rapax was stationed at Strasbourg. In 69, in the first battle of Cremona, it had a bad time with a newly organized legion, I Adiutrix, which even captured its eagle. It did better later in the battle but then made another mistake by not siding with Vespasian. Unlike four other legions that made this mistake, it was not disbanded but instead sent to Bonn. In 85 or 86, XXI Rapax replaced its old enemy, I Adiutrix, at Mainz. In 89, it seems to have revolted again; this time the legion was packed off to Pannonia. It participated in Domitian's campaign against the Sarmatians and disappeared entirely in 92, either destroyed in battle or disbanded.

XXII DEIOTARIANA

Augustus

The name of this legion is unique. Deiotarus, king of Galatia in what is now northern Turkey, organized his troops along Roman lines, and during the time of Caesar, fought campaigns in support of Caesar. The kingdom was bequeathed to Augustus in 25 B.C., and this formation was accepted into the Roman army as a legion bearing the name of its Galatian founder.[5] Prior to 8 B.C., XXII Deiotariana was stationed three miles from Alexandria at Nicopolis, in a fortress built for the legion by Augustus. In 119, it was still in Alexandria (Nicopolis) sharing a camp with II Cyrenaica, which was sent off the following year to Arabia. In 132, the Jewish war started, and XXII Deiotariana disappeared, either destroyed in combat or abolished. It spent virtually its entire career in Egypt in or near Alexandria.

Nine

First-Century Formations

During the reigns of Tiberius, who succeeded Augustus, and Gaius, no new legions were added to the twenty-five that already existed. The first new legions, XV and XXII Primigenia, were raised by Claudius, 41-54, presumably to make other legions available for the invasion of Britain. Nero raised two legions and Galba another, named for himself. Vespasian added three more but also disbanded or removed four from the list. Finally, Domitian added one more. V Alaudae, however, was destroyed in 92, and XXI Rapax disappeared about the same time. Thus, at the close of the first century, there were twenty-eight standing legions. The nine organized by the five later emperors will be discussed in this chapter.

XV PRIMIGENIA

Fortuna

XV Primigenia had a very short and undistinguished career. Organized by Claudius,[1] XV and XXII Primigenia were the first new legions since the death of Augustus A.D. 14. They were named for the goddess of fortune, Fortuna Primigenia. Claudius, with his plans for the invasion of Britain, needed them to replace legions on the Rhine being withdrawn for the British campaign. In 43, XV Primigenia was stationed on the upper Rhine near Mainz. From there, the legion was moved to Bonn. In 69, it joined the revolt against Otho. The legion then found itself being besieged at Vetera (Xanten) by Civilis, who was attempting to form his Gallic empire. The legion surrendered to Civilis, earning the keen displeasure of Vespasian, who shortly thereafter crushed the Civilis revolt. It appears that in 70, Vespasian disbanded its remnants and also three other legions: I Germanicus, IV Macedonica, and XVI Gallica. All four legions were considered to have disgraced themselves.

Plutarch, in his life of Galba, writes, "Most say that he [Galba] was killed by a soldier of Legion XV." As the other legion XV, Apollinaris, was at this time in the East, it may be assumed that XV Primigenia was responsible for the murder.

XXII PRIMIGENIA

Domitian

Formed by Claudius at the same time as XV Primigenia, XXII Primigenia had a long and distinguished career. The goddess Fortuna Primigenia smiled on it. Domitian honored the legion with the additional title *pia fidelis Domitiana,* and at one time it had a future emperor as its commander. Once organized, it was first dispatched to Mainz, where it shared a camp with IV Macedonica. This was about 39, when Claudius was preparing for his conquest of Britain.

XXII Primigenia went off to Italy in 69 to help Vitellius defeat Otho's legions at the first battle of Cremona. Vitellius didn't last long. A few months later, the legion found itself on the wrong side at the second battle of Cremona when the forces of Vespasian defeated those of Vitellius. The legion was then packed off to Pannonia. Vespasian must have thought well of the legion, for he did not abolish it. In 70, XXII Primigenia was back in the Rhine Valley, this time probably at Nijmegen in what is now the Netherlands. The base troops that had remained behind on the Rhine when the legion was in Italy seem to have been wiped out by Civilis during his abortive uprising.

Some time after 84, the double camp at Xanten was replaced by a stone fortress and XXII Primigenia was based there.

In 89, a civil war broke out when Antonius Saturninus, governor of upper Germany, led a revolt against the emperor Domitian. The legions of the upper Rhine followed him, but those of the lower Rhine, including XXII Primigenia, retained their loyalty to the emperor. Maximus, the governor of lower Germany, led his troops against Saturninus and won a major victory against serious odds. The engagement took place on the plain of Andernach between Bonn and Coblenz. German forces that had planned to cross the Rhine to help Saturninus were foiled by a sudden thaw of the frozen river. Later, when Domitian arrived on the scene, he rewarded the loyal legions with the additional title of *pia fidelis Domitiana.* In view of the fact that Saturninus, whose head was sent to Rome, had financed the revolt by using the banks of two legions, Domitian issued an edict setting a limit on how much money could be held in such banks. At this time, he also forbade the stationing of two legions in a single camp.

In 110, reports show the legion in upper Germany. While stationed in Germany, it had as its commander Didius Julianus, who was to be emperor in 193.

A commemorative slab found on the Antonine Wall in Scotland hints that an element of the legion helped in the construction of the wall about 193. No evidence has come to light of the legion having detachments in Britain. In 241, two centuries after its founding, XXII Primigenia was still stationed at Mainz.

I ITALICA

Nero

The emperor Nero liked to do things in the grand manner. Toward the end of his reign, he developed a project to conquer the Caucasus, apparently with some thought of occupying the steppes of southern Russia. At the same time, Nero conceived another plan, to conquer Ethiopia. For the latter campaign, he started to concentrate troops in Alexandria. As one of the steps in preparing for the Caucasus venture, he organized a new legion, I Italica. This legion was to be special, and he established a requirement that all its members be from Italy and all be over six feet tall. He called it "The Phalanx of Alexander the Great." Before either venture could be launched, Galba, Otho, and the praetorian guard all joined in a revolt; and in January 69, Nero committed suicide.

Organization of I Italica, which had started in September 67, had been completed. The legion was concentrated at Lyon in southern France. It got swept up in the Vitellian campaign against Otho. When Vitellius was, in turn, overthrown by the forces of Vespasian, I Italica was sent off to Novae, near present-day Svishtov, in Bulgaria. This general area south of the Danube was the Roman province of Moesia.

The legion, according to reports, seems to have remained based at Novae or nearby Oescus for the next century, for we have reports of it there in 79, 93, 96, 106, 110, and 138. The last report at hand is for the year 200; the legion was still based in lower Moesia, presumably Novae.

It must not be assumed, however, that the legion had a sedentary life. Throughout this period, the tribes north of the Danube were almost continuously at war with the Romans. I Italica participated in the Dacian War of 87, the wars with the Sarmatians, and, during Trajan's time, 98-117,in at least two more wars with the Dacians.

VII GEMINA (GALBIANA)

Trajan

Before leaving Spain to serve his seven months as emperor in Rome, Sulpicius Galba, having been governor of Spain for eight years, raised a new legion, which bore his name, VII Galbiana. Its birth date is given as 10 June 68. The legion went to Rome with the new emperor. After a short stay there, VII Galbiana was posted on the Danube at Carnuntum. It was but a short time before the new emperor, Otho, called the legion back to Italy for his unsuccessful defense against Vitellius at the first battle of Cremona. Then it was back to the Danube again under the orders of Vitellius where it was reorganized, and renamed VII Gemina.

Vespasian, who was still in Alexandria, chose Antonius Primus, the commanding officer of VII Gemina, to organize forces for the takeover of the empire from Vitellius. Undoubtedly still smarting from the defeat at the first battle of Cremona, the legion strongly supported Vespasian and, with other like-minded legions, won the second battle of Cremona. This resulted in the death of Vitellius on 20 December 69, and the elevation of Vespasian. After this victory, it was back again to the station on the Danube.

Once things settled down, Vespasian apparently made a decision to transfer VII Gemina back to Spain. On its way back from the Danube in 73 or 74, VII Gemina was held for several years as part of the army of the upper Rhine. Eventually the legion continued to Spain and was stationed at Leon, a communications center of major importance.

In 89, a revolt broke out in Germany with Antonius Saturninus, governor of upper Germany, having himself proclaimed emperor by the two legions stationed at Mainz. His revolt was short-lived, but at its start, VII Gemina was summoned from Spain by Domitian. Although it moved very rapidly under the command of the future emperor Trajan, the legion arrived too late for the decisive battle on the plain of Andernach. It then returned to Spain with the thanks of the emperor.

Records of the legion after this move are limited. VII Gemina was reported in Spain in 110, 120, 138, 161, and 196. In fact, the Notitia mentions an element of the legion in Spain in the fourth century.

Pertinax

I ADIUTRIX

Nero, in preparing for his projected campaign in the Caucasus, ordered the formation of two new legions, one to be organized using sailors of the Roman fleet. Not only was this source of soldiers unusual, but that they were not Roman citizens was unprecedented. Legion membership provided the soldiers with a means of getting this citizenship. The legion was named I Adiutrix, meaning a reserve or supporting legion "in addition to others." The legion had not been fully organized when Nero died. Some of its members met the emperor Galba on his entrance to Rome and petitioned heatedly for certain privileges; these privileges were denied. Some rioting took place, and several of the legion members were killed.[2] As a result, when Otho overthrew Galba some months later, I Adiutrix was much on the side of Otho. There is a report that Galba had actually ordered the legion decimated for failing to respect his authority.

The legion was strong in support of Otho and fought for him with distinction at the first battle of Cremona. Although Otho's forces finally lost the battle, and Otho subsequently his life, I Adiutrix showed great ability, particularly for a new and untested outfit. In a head-to-head battle with the experienced XXI Rapax, I Adiutrix gave the veterans a very bad time and actually captured their eagle. Before the battle was over, XXI Rapax counterattacked with equal success, but I Adiutrix had established itself as a legion to be reckoned with.

In 70, and again in 83, the legion was based on the Rhine. It, with XIV Gemina, built and occupied a new stone fortress at Mainz. In 85 or 86, it was replaced at Mainz by its old enemy XXI Rapax; I Adiutrix was called by Domitian to Pannonia (Hungary).

Briefly under Trajan, about 106, the legion provided occupation troops in Dacia (Romania). In 108, it was reported at Brigetio, near present-day Komaron, about forty-five miles northwest of Budapest. About this time, the legion was honored with the additional title of *pia fidelis,* indicating special loyalty to Trajan during some unidentified revolt. In 115, elements of the legion were taken by Trajan for his Armenian campaign, but the legion was still reported at Brigetio in 120 and in 138. In 173, under the command of the future emperor Pertinax, I Adiutrix was credited with liberating Raetia and Noricum from invaders. In 216, the legion participated in the Mesopotamian campaign of Caracalla. In 228, it was back on its post on the Danube, presumably at Brigetio.

The legion was last in the limelight about the year 259, when the emperor Gallienus brought it from the Danube to Italy to help repulse an invasion by the Alemanni near Milan. Although part of a relatively small army—estimated at ten thousand men—it administered a crushing defeat to the much larger host of invaders.

II ADIUTRIX

Caracalla

Like I Adiutrix, this legion was organized from sailors of the fleet, from Ravenna this time. Organization was not completed until March 70, when Vespasian incorporated the legion into the nine-legion army he dispatched to put down the revolt being led by Civilis in Germany. After a short stay in Germany on the lower Rhine, II Adiutrix was transferred to Britain, first stationed at Lincoln and then at Chester, where it was reported in 79. It was taken from Britain probably in 86 and sent to the Danube front, where it was more needed. The legion took part in Trajan's Dacian campaign of 86-88 and fought the Suebi in 97. In 95, the nineteen-year-old future emperor Hadrian was a tribune of the legion.

In 105, the legion was at Singidunum (Belgrade). In 106, II Adiutrix moved up the Danube to Aquincum near Budapest. The legion played a part in Trajan's Parthian campaign (Persia) in 113 and then returned to Budapest. In 162 and 163, it participated in another Parthian war, this time during the opening years of the reign of Marcus Aurelius. In the following year, the legion was returned to Budapest, but in 173 it was reported at Trencin, Czechoslovakia, deep in the lands of the Marcomanni. After its successful part in the Marcomanni war, II Adiutrix was once more returned to Budapest in 193. The last report is for the year 216, when Caracalla took it to Mesopotamia for his Parthian campaign. It was returned then to Budapest.

IV FLAVIA FIRMA

Vespasian, the first of the three emperors of the Flavian family, gave the family name to two of the legions he raised in 70. He disbanded four legions, among them XVI Gallica and IV Macedonica; he used their numbers and probably some of their better soldiers in forming XVI Flavia firma and IV Flavia firma.

Vespasian

IV Flavia firma was sent first to Burnum, modern-day Knin, in Dalmatia, Yugoslavia. In 86, the emperor Domitian brought the legion north and east for the war in Dacia. Dalmatia, which had revolted in the first decade, was now quiet, and no legion was required there. The situation was different in Dacia, which had been causing trouble since the last century B.C. Raiding had been taking place over the Danube from the north all along the river from Vienna to the Black Sea. In 85-86, under their powerful leader Decebalus, the Dacians were again raiding over the Danube into Moesia and were driven back by Roman troops. The Romans, however, suffered a serious defeat in Dacia. Yet in 88, Domitian's legions, presumably including IV Flavia firma, won a major victory in Dacia itself. The legion was then stationed at Belgrade (Singidunum) and undoubtedly took part in Trajan's successful war against the Dacians in 106. Reports show IV Flavia firma on the Danube in 108 and in 120. It appears to have remained in this part of Moesia, either at Belgrade or fifty miles away at Viminacium, during the entire next two centuries.

XVI FLAVIA FIRMA

Macrinus

Like IV Flavia firma, XVI Flavia firma was organized by Vespasian in the year 70. The legion bore his family name, with the quality of being steadfast added. Unlike IV Flavia firma, which was first stationed in Europe, XVI Flavia firma was initially established at Satala in northeast Turkey. Its history seems to be bound up with the East, whereas its sister legion was always in Europe. It formed a part of Trajan's army that made the grand sweep down the Tigris and Euphrates rivers in 114-115. Trajan then established XVI Flavia firma at Samosata, now known as Samsat, in southeast Turkey. This locale is a key crossing of the Euphrates and had to be secure for any Roman operations in the area. During Hadrian's reign, 117-138, XVI Flavia firma and VI Ferrata were together the garrison of Samosata. In 138, the legion was reported in Syria, but shortly thereafter it was back at Samosata.

In 197 and 198, XVI Flavia firma was part of the emperor Severus's army that captured Ctesiphon, the Parthian capital south of present-day Baghdad. In 216, the legion was again taken from Samosata, this time by Caracalla, for his Parthian campaign in Mesopotamia.

XVI Flavia firma was undoubtedly part of the army that the emperor Macrinus put together in 217 for his unsuccessful Parthian campaign. In 218, the emperor was killed when resisting the forces of Elagabalus from his base in Antioch. Elagabalus then became emperor.

Severus had the legion in his ten-legion concentration. In 231, he based himself at Antioch for his retaliatory campaign against the rising power of Persia. Under its new and effective leader, Ardashir, Persia was challenging the empire. This campaign was not a success for either side. The records do not show in which of the columns the legion marched.

The legion returned again to Samosata, but in 260 it was withdrawn to western Turkey.

I MINERVIA

The last new legion to be formed in the first century was I Minervia, organized by Domitian in 83 and named for the emperor's patron goddess. The requirement for more troops on the Danube for the Chatti campaign had caused the withdrawal of XXI Rapax from Bonn; the new I Minervia took its place there.

Minerva

In 89, the legion demonstrated its loyalty to the emperor when the governor of the upper Rhine, Saturninus, led a revolt. Saturninus utilized the two legions at Mainz, XIV Gemina and XXI Rapax, which had returned from the Danube. I Minervia, with the other lower Rhine legions, supported the emperor, and the revolt was short-lived. As a result, I Minervia received the additional honorific title *pia fidelis Domitiana.*

Other results of this uprising were the prompt transfer of XXI Rapax back to the Danube, to be followed there two years later by its unsuccesful comrade-in-arms, XIV Gemina. At this time, Domitian issued the edict against stationing two legions together in the same camp. The emperor also set the limit on the amount of money that could be held in the legion banks.

In the winter of 102-103, I Minervia was moved to the Danube for Trajan's campaign against the Dacians. Hadrian commanded the legion in Trajan's successful campaign, which resulted in the capture of the Dacian capital.

It was indeed a fortunate legion that had a commander such as Hadrian. Hadrian was a Greek scholar, athlete, soldier at fourteen, administrator, legion tribune at nineteen, legion commander at thirty, and a poet of some ability. He was emperor at forty-two. His quips are still quoted by scholars.[3] He, unlike other emperors, died a natural death in 138 at the age of sixty, having just composed a poem to his soul.

By 110, I Minervia had been returned to the Rhine. It was again reported at Bonn in 120 and 138.

In 162, the legion made its only expedition to the East when Emperor Marcus Aurelius used it in his highly successful war against the Parthians. The Parthian leader, Osroes, had taken over control of Armenia and had scattered the somewhat less energetic eastern legions while capturing much of Syria. Marcus Aurelius took his Rhine and Danube legions to Syria and completely defeated Osroes, restoring the Roman position in that part of the world.

By 166, the legion was back at its base at Bonn and was reported still in upper Germany in 200. In 231, I Minervia was given the difficult task of holding back the Franks, who were pushing hard on the Rhine frontier.

Ten

Second-Century Formations

During the second century, seven new legions were organized: two at the start of the century by Trajan, two in mid-century by Marcus Aurelius, and three just at the close of the century by Septimius Severus. By the beginning of the third century, however, two Augustan legions, IX Hispana and XXII Deiotariana, were destroyed or disbanded. Thus, in the first decade of the third century, there were thirty-three legions in being, four more than at the start of the second century.

During the last part of the second century and the beginning of the third, there continued the shift, mentioned in Chapter Five, of legions from the west and north to the east and south. An examination of the order of battle maps for 130 and 230 shows that although the numbers of legions had increased by two, the number on the Rhine had decreased from five to four. The number on the Danube had, during the same period, increased from ten to twelve, and in the Middle East, from eight to ten.

II TRAIANA

Maximinus

When the emperor Trajan had settled things in Rome, he looked to the problem of Dacia that he inherited from Domitian and Nerva. His first move was to raise two new legions, one of them II Traiana. Dacia had a strong leader, Decebalus, who united the forces of his kingdom. Two campaigns were required before Dacia could be conquered. II Traiana was certainly part of the second campaign. In 110, the legion was reported in upper Moesia, holding one of the strong points on the Danube on the south border of Dacia.

In 114, Trajan had the legion available for his Armenian campaign and his subsequent drive down through Mesopotamia to the Persian Gulf. Records do not show what part the legion played in this campaign.

Further reports show the legion in Egypt in 120, 135, and 194; and at Nicopolis near Alexandria in 231. In 232, the commanding officer of the legion was Gaius Julius Verus Maximinus, a giant soldier who had risen from the ranks and achieved the rank of centurion under Caracalla. After commanding the legion, Maximinus went on to be supreme commander of the Roman armies. In 235, he became emperor and ruled for three years. During the seige of Aquileia, which had espoused the cause of the next emperor, Gordian, he was murdered in his tent by troops of II Parthica.

In 232, when Maximinus was in command, the legion had a detachment in Syria that participated in a small and unsuccessful revolt. The last report of the legion is for the year 288, when Diocletian sent a major portion of it on the expedition from Tangier to Carthage to resecure that part of the empire.

XXX ULPIA VICTRIX

Trajan

The second of the two legions formed by Trajan was given the number XXX. Organized in response to the needs of the Dacian War, XXX Ulpia Victrix became, in 101, the thirtieth active legion in the army. Having given his dynastic name to the first legion he formed, II Traiana, he gave the family name, Ulpius, to this new legion. The family had a distinguished military background. Trajan's father, M. Ulpius Trajanus, had commanded V Macedonica at the siege and capture of Jerusalem. Trajan himself had commanded VII Gemina in 89 when they rushed from Spain to the Rhineland to help Domitian put down Saturninus's revolt.

After the Dacian campaign, XXX Ulpia Victrix was reported at Sarmzegetus in Dacia (near Vulcan in Transylvania). In 110, the legion had moved south to upper Moesia, probably on the Danube. From there, it was taken by Trajan for his Armenian campaign. By 119, the legion had been transferred to lower Germany at Vetera, present-day Xanten. There it replaced VI Victrix, which had been rushed to Britain to put down a serious revolt.

At this point, records of the legion become almost nonexistent, but there is one report that shows it in upper Germany in 138. A final report for 269 shows the legion still at Vetera, having retained its headquarters for a century and a half at the same location.

II ITALICA PIA

Marcus Aurelius

Marcus Aurelius, emperor of Rome, 161-180, was a scholar, statesman, philosopher, athlete, author, and soldier. Unlike other emperors, he did not find it necessary to name new legions after himself. Instead, he named them for his native land,[1] and II Italica Pia (patriotic) was the first to be formed. It was called into being because of the desperate situation both on the Danube and in Parthia (Persia). Rome was usually able to arrange to have one war at a time, but Marcus inherited two at once. It is regrettable that he preferred to write philosophy rather than history, for there are few records of the legions during the last half of the second century. II Italica was raised either in 165 or 166 when the plague was sweeping through the Roman army. In 169, records show the legion in Germany on the Danube at Casta Regina (Regensburg). After 170, it was reported at Lauriacum near Linz, Austria, one hundred miles to the east but still on the Danube. It probably served in the Parthian War, but dates are not available.

When Marcus Aurelius died at Vindobonna (Vienna) in 180, II Italica Pia was back on the Danube, at or near Regensburg. In 253, the legion is reported in Noricum, so it may well have been at its old base at Lauriacum. From

Noricum, it was taken back to Italy by the emperor Gallienus for his famous victory in 258; with outnumbered forces, he crushed the Alemanni near Milan.

III ITALICA CONCORS

In addition to II Italica, Marcus Aurelius raised a second legion, III Italica Concors, the "concors" implying concordant, harmonious, and efficient.

When the organization of the legion was complete in 166, it was sent initially to the north of Italy to defend that frontier.

Marcus Aurelius

Although records are very scarce, there is indication that it was moved briefly to Germany and then went to the Parthian War with II Italica. By 170, it was reported in Noricum, which is roughly present-day Austria. There are two reports of III Italica Concors then being stationed at or near Regensburg, where it seems to have remained until at least the beginning of the third century.

In 216, the emperor Caracalla took the legion to Mesopotamia for his Parthian campaign and presumably returned it to the Regensburg area thereafter.

I PARTHICA

Septimius Severus became emperor in 193 and immediately formed three new legions, I, II, and III Parthica. The first and third were organized in the East in what was then Mesopotamia. I Parthica was first stationed at Nisibis near the modern town of Al Qamishli on Syria's northeast border.

Septimus Severus

After a very brief stay in Rome, Severus departed for Syria, where some legions had indicated support for C. Pescennius Niger's bid to be Rome's ruler. Earlier, Severus had himself commanded a legion in Syria.

The army that Severus put together may well have included the new I Parthica. In any event, the defeat and death of Niger were accomplished in 194. Byzantium held out, however, against Severus until 196, when he captured and destroyed the city and demolished its then-famous wall. The principal inhabitants were put to the sword. In 198, the legion is again reported at Nisibis.

In 231, a report shows the legion having moved to Singara, a hundred miles to the southeast and about thirty miles from present-day Al Mawsil. Although it can be presumed to have participated in the successive wars with Parthia, no actual record is available.

The last firm report concerning the legion is for the year 231. I Parthica was still at Singara and participated with III Parthica in a mutiny that cost the governor of the province his life.

II PARTHICA

Gordian

Organized by Septimius Severus in 193, this legion, unlike its sisters I and III Parthica that were formed in the East, was established at Albano, some twenty miles south of Rome. It would appear that the emperor wished to have troops that he could count on near the capital.

It is not known whether II Parthica was part of the force used by Severus when he defeated Clodius Albinus, the candidate for the purple who brought his legions from Britain and Gaul. The battle took place in 197 at Lyon. Although there is no evidence to prove it, the strategic location of II Parthica would certainly indicate that it participated in the victory.

The legion is listed as one of those that participated in Caracalla's Parthian campaign in Mesopotamia in 216. In 218, it joined forces with III Gallica at Raphanaea in supporting Elagabalus's bid for the empire. Its success in the battle south of Antioch won for it the title *pia fidelis felix aeterna*.

In 238, II Parthica was back in Italy and participated in the siege of Aquileia, near Monfalcone, on the Gulf of Venice. The emperor, Maximinus, was attempting to capture the city that had gone over to the Gordian claimant to the empire. Troops from II Parthica murdered Maximinus and his son in their tent, thus winning praise from the Gordian followers.

In 258, the legion returned to its base at Albano. It was quickly taken from there by the emperor Gallienus, who put an army together to hold against the Alemanni. This German force had penetrated well into Italy. Gallienus, although he had fewer troops, completely defeated the Alemanni at Milan. The enemy was virtually destroyed, and the remnants were chased out of Italy. After this battle, the legion returned to Albano.

III PARTHICA

Valerian

The story of III Parthica is much the same as that of its sister legion, I Parthica. Both were formed by Septimius Severus in 193. Both had their first station at Nisibis in Mesopotamia. Both were participants in the successful wars of Severus against the Persians.

Shortly before 231, the legion moved with I Parthica to Singara, one hundred miles to the south. There it helped prove the correctness of the injunction of Emperor Domitian, issued about 84, against stationing two legions in the same place at the same time. The two Parthica legions revolted in 231 and killed the governor of the province. Unlike the case of I Parthica, we do have a general report concerning this legion's demise. In 235, it was a functioning legion; but in 284, it no longer existed.[2] Lacking available records, it must be assumed that both III and I Parthica were destroyed when Mesopotamia was overrun by the Persians in the campaigns of 230, 241, 256, and 260. It was in this last year that the emperor Valerian was captured at Edessa by the Persian leader Shapur. The emperor was to die in captivity shortly thereafter. In 241, Nisibis, the birthplace of the legion, had fallen to the Persians.

At the time of III Parthica's demise, the structure of the Roman legion was changing fast. The emperors were more often using detachments from various legions rather than the legions themselves as fighting units. By the year 300, few legions remained intact with the morale and capabilities of the legions of the first two centuries.

The praetorian guard can be said to have gone out with a bang at the battle of Milvian Bridge. The legions, however, did not go out with a whimper; in the words of MacArthur, like old soldiers, they just faded away.

Throughout its history, the guard was essentially a democracy wrapped in a dictatorship. One didn't command the men in the castra to accept new emperors or dispose of old ones. One went to the castra and presented one's case, not to the tribunes alone, but to the guard assembled. If the guard acclaimed you, the empire was yours. If they refused you, your future was questionable. All in all, the guard helped to establish ten emperors. During the same period, twelve emperors were dethroned by the praetorians.[1] The praetorians were taller, stronger, better dressed, and better paid than most Romans. They were picked men who carried themselves with style as an elite.[2] This did not endear them to the civilian population nor to the literary coterie who wrote the histories.

In the field, the praetorians were superb soldiers. Their very self-confidence made them so. They had an intense loyalty to their own and to their standards. This loyalty did not always extend to their prefects or to the emperors who appointed them.

While the guard was an elite corps attached to the person of the emperor, the legions were the main battle force of the empire. After the third century, however, the legions lost their preeminence. Diocletian, toward the end of that century, increased the number of legions from roughly thirty to over sixty, but the strength of the legions was greatly reduced, as were their capabilities for countering enemy incursions.

Although the names and numbers of the majority of the legions survived well into the fourth century, they were no longer employed in the same manner as in the great days of the empire.

132

The change was gradual but in due course the role of the legion as a counterattacking force was almost eliminated. During the first three centuries, the legions were used as a distributed reserve. The auxiliary troops manned the frontiers, and a legion was called only when the auxiliary troops could no longer handle a situation. Quite often the legion not only restored the situation, but also invaded the enemy area and cut the former raiding force to pieces. During the earlier centuries, the legions were moved along the support area to the east or south as needed. They constituted a close-up mobile reserve.

In the fourth century, central reserve forces were established, made up largely of cavalry and usually under the direct control of the emperor. Although many considered this an improved concept, it may well have been exactly the reverse. The still stirrup-less cavalry could move faster than the legions but normally had much greater distances to cover. They were not as easily moved by water and, in some cases, would have to take land routes when legions would have gone by a direct water route. With auxiliary units manning the defenses, the legions were usually free to move rapidly to endangered areas. For short moves, legions could cover considerably more than twenty miles a day.

A critical situation at Bonn on the Rhine could call forward three legions in three days and a fourth in another four. Similarly, at Carnuntum, three legions could make the march in two days, and a third legion could be there three days later. It is unlikely that a central reserve would even have heard about the problem by the time the legions reached the area. Even on the much less strongly held Euphrates front, an incursion between Samosata and Melitene could be met within three days by two legions, and a third would be on the scene in eight days. It would be weeks, or more likely months, before a central reserve could appear.

It is also questionable whether forces made up largely of cavalry were as effective as the legions. Enemy tactics had not changed, and one recalls that III Gallica had little trouble destroying a force of nine thousand Sarmatian cavalry in 69. Similarly, a ten-thousand-man army assembled by Gallienus from I Adiutrix, II Parthica, II Italica, VIII Augusta, and the praetorian guard defeated and destroyed a much larger force of invading Alemanni at Milan in 258-259.

The great strength and effectiveness of both the legions and the guard lay in their training, morale, and leadership. Training obviously suffered when the legions were broken up and used in defensive positions. Attack training must have suffered most severely. Morale was generally high in the first three centuries, and the legions believed strongly in themselves. Also, in the early years, the high rank of the legion commanders led to self-confidence in the troops, for they knew that they were a power in the empire. So did the emperor. Ten legion commanders used their legions as springboards and became, themselves, emperors. The soldiers and centurions, when serving an emperor who had himself served in or commanded a legion, were conscious of their might. To what degree the reduction of the legions' power and effectiveness was a result of imperial fear of the legions is not clear. This fear, however, must have played a significant part in the weakening of the empire.

In the centuries when the legions were at their prime, there was a unique esprit de corps unrelated to pay, skill, training, or technical leadership. A willingness to die for the empire existed among the troops and their leaders. There was, in addition, a personal honor that required success and did not permit failure.

Emperors, centurions, and legion commanders killed themselves when they failed in their tasks. The centurion Sempronius Densus, alone defending his emperor from the rebel troops in Rome, was not an isolated example. Neither was the suicide of Poenius Postumas, acting commander of II Augusta, when he failed to bring the legion into the battle against Boudicca. This concept of the honor of the soldier has been found in other countries at other times but seldom over such a length of time as was found in the guard and the legions.

Author's Preface

1. *Julius Caesar*, act 3, sc. 2, lines 80-81.
2. Major modern army headquarters maintain order of battle sections that keep military histories of significant enemy units.

Chapter One

1. General Dwight Eisenhower had the First United States Infantry Division under his command in Africa, Sicily, and at the Normandy invasion. On 4 July 1944, Eisenhower called the division his "praetorian guard."
2. The four praetorian prefects who later became emperors were Titus Flavius Sabinus Vespasian (69-79), Marcus Opellius Macrinus (217-18), Marcus Julius Philippus (244), and Marcus Aurelius Carus (282-83).
3. The coinage of Augustus included the denarius, a silver coin, and the gold Aureus, equal in value to twenty-five denarii. Inflation was continuous during the early centuries of our era. Thus, the purchasing power of the coinage is difficult to estimate. The base pay of a soldier in the legions of Augustus was roughly one denarius a day. In the East, payment was made with the drachma, a silver coin of the same weight and value as the denarius.
4. See Tacitus, *The Histories*, trans. Kenneth Wellesley (New York: Penguin Books, 1975), II. 39-45.
5. See Kenneth Wellesley, *The Long Year A.D. 69* (Boulder, Colo.: Westview Press, 1976), p. 99.
6. See Naphtali Lewis and Meyer Reinhold, *Roman Civilization Sourcebook II: The Empire* (New York: Harper Torchbooks, 1966), p. 129.

Chapter Two

1. Herodian, *The History*, trans. C.R. Whittaker (Cambridge, Mass.: Harvard University Press, 1969), I. 16, 17.4.
2. See Will Durant, *Caesar and Christ* (New York: Simon & Schuster, 1944), p. 352.
3. See Herodian, *The History*, IV. 6.4-7.
4. Ibid., IV. 7.7.
5. Ibid., IV. 9.4-7.
6. This account of Elagabalus's victory is the author's interpretation of the descriptions offered by Dio and Herodian.

Chapter Three

1. See *Scriptores Historiae Augustae* [hereafter referred to as *Augustan History*] (Cambridge, Mass.: Harvard University Press, 1922), Elagabalus XVII-XIX for another version of the killing of Elagabalus.

135

2. Alexander came to Rome with the name Alexius Bassianus. In 221, he was adopted as the successor to Elagabalus and his name was changed to Marcus Aurelius Alexander Severus. He is known as Alexander Severus in most histories.
3. See Herodian, *The History*, VI. 5-6 for a detailed account of this campaign.
4. See Herodian, *The History*, VII. 11-12.
5. See *Augustan History* Gordians XXIX for additional praises of Timesitheus.
6. See *Augustan History* Claudius XV for mention of Murena, Probus IV for Gallicanus, and Aurelian XIII for Macer.
7. For a description of Placidianus's career, see L.L. Howe, *The Praetorian Prefect, from Commodus to Diocletian* (Chicago: University of Chicago Press, 1942), p. 82.
8. Ibid., pp. 92-93.
9. In the West, the emperors were Maxentius, Maximian, and Constantine; in the East, Licinius, Maximin, and Galerius.
10. Grossly exaggerated strengths for the armies of Constantine and Maxentius are given in Edward Gibbon, *The Decline and Fall of the Roman Empire* (New York: Cerf and Klopfer, 1932), vol. 1, p. 360.
11. Assuming that there were still four urban cohorts, a prudent commander would have kept two in Rome as security against an uprising in the city or a raid by Constantine's cavalry.
12. Another portrayal of the battle of the Milvian Bridge is found in Gibbon, *Decline and Fall*, p. 365.

Chapter Four

1. See Lewis and Reinhold, *Roman Civilization*, pp. 527-39 for retirement rights, including directives of Domitian and Constantine. See also David J. Breeze and Brian Dobson, *Hadrian's Wall* (New York: Penguin Books, 1976), p. 190.
2. See H.M.D. Parker, *The Roman Legions* (New York: Barnes & Noble, 1958), pp. 193-94.
3. John 19:28-30.
4. Mark 15:39.
5. See Breeze and Dobson, *Hadrian's Wall*, p. 186.
6. See Anthony Birley, *Life in Roman Britain* (London: Batsford Ltd., 1964), p. 46.
7. Addressing the chief centurions of the legion, Hadrian pointed out that despite the absence of a detached cohort and other troops, the centurions had performed well and deserved his commendation. He congratulated the legion cavalry not only for its spirit but also for its performance in the most difficult of all exercises—javelin throwing when clad in armor. The attached cavalry cohort won special praise for its rapid construction of a stone fortification and for its combat maneuvers. Hadrian praised the First Company of Pannonians for their throwing of the javelin and lance and gave them largess. The hurling of stones with slings and close-knit maneuver won praise for the cavalry of the Sixth Cohort of Commagenians. See Lewis and Reinhold, *Roman Civilization*, pp. 507-9.
8. Tacitus, *The Histories*, III. 1-35.

Chapter Five

1. Plutarch describes the incident as follows in *The Lives of the Noble Grecians and Romans* (New York: Modern Library), "Galba," p. 1284: Galba got into his chair and was carried out to sacrifice to Jupiter, and so to show himself publicly. But coming into the forum, there met him there, like a turn of wind, the opposite story, that Otho had made himself master of the camp. And as usual in a crowd of such a size, some called to him to return back, others to move forwards; some encouraged him to be bold and fear nothing, others bade him to be cautious and distrust. And thus whilst his chair was tossed to and fro, as it were on the waves, often tottering, there appeared first horse, and straightway heavy-armed foot, coming through Paulus's court, and all with one accord crying out, "Down with this private man." Upon this, the crowd of people set off running, not to fly and disperse, but to possess themselves of the colonnades and elevated places of the forum, as it might be to get places to see a spectacle. And as soon as Atillius Vergilio knocked down one of Galba's statues, this was taken as the declaration of war, and they sent a discharge of darts upon Galba's litter, and missing their aim, came up and attacked him nearer hand with their naked swords. No man resisted or offered to stand up in his defence, save one only, a centurion, Sempronius Densus, the single man among so many thousands that the sun beheld that day act worthily of the Roman empire who, though he had never received any favour from Galba, yet out of bravery and allegiance endeavoured to defend the litter. First, lifing up his switch of vine, with which the centurions correct the soldiers when disorderly, he called aloud to the aggressors, charging them not to touch their emperor. And when they came upon him hand-to-hand, he drew his sword, and made a defence for a long time, until at last he was cut under the knees and brought to the ground. Galba's chair was upset at the spot called the Lacus Curtius, where they ran up and struck at him as he lay in his corselet. He, however, offered his throat, bidding them "Strike, if it be for the Romans' good." He received several wounds on his legs and arms, and at last was struck in the throat, as most say, by one Camurius, a soldier of the fifteenth legion.
2. See Cassius Dio, *Roman History*, trans. Earnest Cary, vols. 7-8 (Cambridge, Mass.: Harvard University Press, 1924), LXIII. 1-12.
3. See Tacitus, *The Agricola and the Germania*, trans. H. Mattingly and S.A. Handford (New York: Penguin Books, 1970), 28-38.
4. See Tacitus, *The Annals of Imperial Rome*, trans. Michael Grant (New York: Penguin Books, 1956), p. 46.
5. Mons Graupius has never been precisely located.
6. See Parker, *The Roman Legions*, p. 161. See also Breeze and Dobson, *Hadrian's Wall*, p. 29.

Chapter Six

1. See Josephus, *The Jewish War*, trans. G.A. Williamson (New York: Penguin Books, 1959), p. 163.
2. Tacitus, *Annals*, p. 106.
3. Mark 6:21-28.

Chapter Seven

1. See Tacitus, *The Histories*, I. 79.
2. See Tacitus, *The Histories*, III. 24-25; see also Dio, *Roman History*, I. LXIV.14.
3. See S.A. Cook, F.E. Adcock, and M.P. Charlesworth, eds., *Cambridge Ancient History* (Cambridge: Cambridge University Press, 1939), vol. 12, p. 84.
4. See L. Carrington Goodrich, *A Short History of the Chinese People* (New York: Harper Torchbooks, 1963), p. 52.
5. See Graham Webster, *The Roman Imperial Army of the First and Second Centuries A.D.* (New York: Funk & Wagnalls, 1969), p. 119.

Chapter Eight

1. See Tacitus, *Annals*, I. 40-44.
2. See Dio, *Roman History*, LXII, Loeb, VIII, pp. 83-105.
3. See Lewis and Reinhold, *Roman Civilization*, pp. 507-9.
4. For an account of the Varian disaster, see Dio, *Roman History*, LVI, Loeb, VII, pp. 39-51.
5. For more on the founding of this legion, see Parker, *The Roman Legions*, pp. 271-72.

Chapter Nine

1. Authorities disagree as to whether XV Primigenia was organized by Claudius or by Gaius.
2. See Plutarch, *Lives*, n.d., p. 1278.
3. In *Lives of the Later Caesars*, trans. Anthony Birley (New York: Penguin Books, 1976), 15:11, the poet Florus is quoted as saying in a poem that he does not want to be Caesar and be among the Britains and in the frosty weather of Scythia. Hadrian replied in his poem that he does not want to be Florus in the taverns and cookshops, putting up with the round insects.

Chapter Ten

1. The family of Marcus Aurelius was originally Spanish, from Uccubi, a chartered town. His great-grandfather had come to Rome and had held the rank of praetor in the Senate.
2. See Edward N. Luttwak, *The Grand Strategy of the Roman Empire From the First Century A.D. to the Third* (Baltimore, Md.: Johns Hopkins University Press, 1976; paperback, 1969), p. 175.

Epilogue

1. Emperors who owed their elevation to the praetorians include Claudius, Nero, Galba, Otho, Domitian, Didius Julianus, Alexander, Gordian III, Tacitus, and Maxentius. Those whose demise is attributable to the praetorians or their prefects include Nero, Galba, Commodus, Pertinax, Julianus, Caracalla, Elagabalus, Maximinus, Maximus, Balbinus, Gordian III, and Gallienus.

2. As used in this study, the word "style" has a meaning close to but not exactly that of the dictionary definition. In general usage, style connotes the manner in which a thing is done rather than the substance of the thing itself. Here the word is used to include both the manner of doing and also to some degree the substance of what is done. In the main, it refers to an attribute of conduct over a period of time, rather than to single isolated actions.

Style is difficult to define precisely for it is a form of character reflected in appearance and conduct that we all recognize without conscious effort. In this sense it is not related to "stylish," nor is it a matter of dress, though dress may reflect it. Nor is style a primarily female quality; probably more males have and have had style than females.

One way of defining the word is to name some individuals who have or have had it. With two exceptions, no president of the United States in this century has had style. The two exceptions are John Kennedy and Franklin Roosevelt, both of whom reflected in the handling of their bodies a self-respect and self-confidence that was recognized generally even by those of us who did not always think well of their conduct in office. One has to go all the way back to Dolley Madison to find in the White House a woman to whom this quality was attributed.

Among the British leadership the quality is equally rare. Sir Anthony Eden, Churchill, and Mountbatten all had this quality but otherwise one looks for it in vain among modern royalty or political leaders. One thinks, of course, of Lady Astor, in modern times. In history there are a few examples, such as Mary Queen of Scots, Elizabeth I, and Victoria. Some would say that Edward VII had it to some degree. Pitt and Disraeli seem to have had it.

The word is not to be confused with charm or with ability, although often an individual had all three. It is certainly not a matter of costume, though again many with style dressed well. The boxing champion Muhammad Ali had it wearing trunks and Duke Kohanamoko similarly garbed, certainly had it. From all descriptions, Kamehameha I showed great style not diminished by his feather cloak.

It is somewhat rare to find husband and wife both with style, but four examples come to mind. Both Lady Mountbatten and Lady Churchill had their own styles. In the theater one thinks of Alfred Lunt and Lynn Fontaine. In Rome's imperial time, if one can believe Tacitus, both Germanicus and his wife, Agrippina I, granddaughter of Augustus, had style that markedly influenced those around them. Although history does not always record the traits that make up style, one can believe that Alexander the Great had it.

Among the military, style is abetted by tradition and uniform, but it is still a rare quality not generally found among successful leaders. One thinks of Robert E. Lee and George Pickett as having style, but not Grant or McClellan. In World War II Field Marshal Alexander and General MacArthur certainly had style. The manner of Patton and Montgomery was unfortunately overladen with a brashness not commensurate with true style. Similarly, the overweening pride of Charles De Gaulle would seem to preclude him. Among the French, one has to go back to Talleyrand and Richelieu to find outstanding examples.

Style, however, is not limited to individuals. It also applies to a way of action or manner of conduct of groups of people in a structured activity. A military funeral usually has great style, though often those participating may have little or no personal style. Similarly, a retreat parade at Fort Myer or at the Marine Barracks in Washington has ritualistic style that impresses one no matter how many times the ceremony has been seen. The same can be said of the changing of the guard at Buckingham Palace.

Like military ceremony, the ceremony of the church with its ancient ritual has style of this second type. The consecration of a bishop, the coronation of a British monarch, and often the celebration of a High Mass or a festival communion take on the quality of style. The rich vestments, silver and gold service, religious music, and often the cathedral environment enhance the style of these religious activities, making them commensurate with military ceremonials.

A third aspect of style reflects both the individual and ceremonial but applies to people in institutions that have over the years continuing ritualistic and ceremonial activities reflect-ing style. Such institutions do not find fertile soil in democracies, and one looks for them in vain in the United States, Switzerland, Republican France, or Mexico. Monarchy is better soil. The House of Lords, the Coldstream Guards, the Vatican as an institution, all have style whether or not the Lord Chancellor, the Regimental Commander, or the current Pope have personal style. The style of the institution rubs off on those who are part of the organization or structure. Individuals who are part of such organizations probably consciously carry themselves and tend to comport themselves with the style of the organization of which they are a part.

It is this third aspect of style, which one might call corporate style, that was to be found in the praetorian guard. The officers and men of the guard conducted themselves with self-confidence and self-respect and in a manner that reflected the guard's composite image of itself. It was not what the guardsmen did but the way they did it that established the style reflected in the individual praetorians. During the three centuries that Rome considered itself the capital of the world, the guard considered itself and conducted itself as the primary military power of that Rome. It is appropriate that when the empire fragmented, the guard was abolished.

Rulers of Rome,
27 B.C. to A.D. 312

B.C.
- 27 Augustus

A.D.
- 14 Tiberius
- 37 Gaius (Caligula)
- 41 Claudius
- 54 Nero
- 68 Galba
- 69 Otho
  Vitellius
  Vespasian
- 79 Titus
- 81 Domitian
- 96 Nerva
- 98 Trajan
- 117 Hadrian
- 138 Antonius Pius
- 161 Marcus Aurelius
- 180 Commodus
- 193 Pertinax
  Didius Julianus
  Septimus Severus
- 211 Caracalla
- 217 Macrinus

- 218 Elagabalus
- 222 Alexander Severus
- 235 Maximinus
- 238 The two Gordiana
  Maximus and Balbinus
  Gordian III
- 244 Philip
- 249 Decius
- 251 Gallus
- 253 Valerian
  Gallienus
- 259 Gallienus, alone
- 268 Claudius II
- 270 Quintillus
  Aurelian
- 275 Tacitus
- 276 Probus
- 282 Carus
- 283 Carinus
- 284 Diocletian (Maximian associated with him, 286)
- 305 Galerius
- 306-312 Maxentius

Chronological List
Of Praetorian Prefects

Omitted from this list are those prefects who did not serve in Rome or who did not serve with cohorts elsewhere in the empire. The four prefects marked with an asterisk are questionable.

Publius Salvius Aper. Appointed by Augustus A.D. 2.
Quintus Ostorius Scapula. Appointed by Augustus to serve with Aper.
Valerius Ligur. Replaced Aper and Scapula.
Lucius Seius Strabo. Replaced Ligur in 14.
Lucius Aelius Sejanus. 14-31; Strabo's son.
Naevius Sutorius Macro. 31-38; committed suicide at Caligula's order.
Rufrius Crispinus. ?-51; removed by Agrippina.
Lusius Geta. ?-51; removed by Agrippina.
Rufrius Pollio. Executed by Claudius.
Cantonius Justus. Joint prefect with Pollio.
Sextus Afranius Burrus. 51-62; selected by the empress.
L. Faenius Rufus. 62-65; executed on Nero's orders.
Scipulus. Killed in 68 by guards who had abandoned Nero.
Gaius Otonius Tigillinus. 62-68; executed in 69.
Nymphidius Sabinus. 65-68; led the revolt against Nero.
Cornelius Laco. Killed in 69.
Plotius Firmus. Appointed by Otho in 69.
Licinius Proculus. An Otho prefect in 69.
Pollio. Appointed by Otho in 69.
Publius Sabinus. Appointed by Vitellius in 69.
Julius Piscus. Appointed by Vitellius in 69.
Alfenus Varus. Appointed by Vitellius in 69 to replace Sabinus.
Marcus Arrecinus Clemens. Served briefly in 69; brother-in-law of Titus.

Titus Flavius Sabinus. 69-79; sole prefect for his father, Vespasian.

Tiberius Julius Alexander. Vespasian appointment; briefly served about 69 as reward for legal service.

Lucius Julius Ursus. Promoted to senatorial rank in 83 by Domitian.

Lucius Laberius Maximus. Appointed in 84 to replace Ursus.

Cornelis Fuscus. Killed in Dacian campaign in 86 or 87.

Casperius Aelianus. Appointed about 85 by Domitian; served under Nerva, and was executed by Trajan in 98.

Norbanus. In 97, participated in the murder of Domitian.

Petronius Secundus. Participated in murder of Domitian; killed by guard in 98.

Saburanus. Named by Trajan.

Claudius Livianus. In Dacian campaigns with Trajan in 101 and 105.

Ameilius Attianus. Coguardian of Hadrian; retired by Hadrian in 117.

C. Sulpicius Similis. Retired by Hadrian about 117.

Marcus Turbo. Appointed 117 to replace Attianus.

C. Septicius Clarus. Hadrian's appointee in 117 to replace Similis; dismissed because of his attentions to the empress.

Gavius Maximus. 135-155; replaced Clarus.

Tatius Maximus. Replaced Gavius Maximus in 155 as sole prefect.

Furius Victorinus. Killed in a battle against the Germans in 168.

Bassaeus Rufus. 169-72.

Macrinius Vindex. Killed in 169 in the German War.

Cornelius Repentinus. Appointed before 180; served both Marcus Aurelius and Commodus.

Tarrutienus Paternus. Appointed before 180; executed about 182.

Tigidius Perennis. 180-85; sole prefect; executed at Commodus's order.

P. Atilius Aebutianus. 185-87; killed at Cleander's order.

Marcus Aurelian Cleander. 187-89; he and both of his sons were executed at Commodus's order.

L. Julius Vehilius Grafus Julianus. Killed by Commodus in 190.

T. Longaeus Rufus. Former prefect of Egypt; killed by Commodus in 190.

Motilenus. Appointed after 190; fed poisoned figs by Commodus.

Marcus Quartus. 190; prefect for five days.

Pescennius Niger. 189 or 190; prefect for six hours.

Quintes Aemilius Laetus. 191-93; arranged the killing of Commodus.

Tullius Crispinus. Killed by Severus's troops in 193.

T. Flavius Genialis. 193-200.

Veturius Macrinus. 193-200; Severus follower appointed by Julianus.

Flavius Juvenalis. 193-97; colleague of Plautianus.

C. Fulvius Plautianus. 197-205; Severus's father-in-law; killed in 205 for plotting against Severus and Caracalla.

A. Amelius Saturninus. Killed by Plautianus in 200.

Amelius Papinianus. 205-11; famous jurist.

Valerius Patrinus. Killed by Caracalla in 211.

A. Maecius Laetus. 205-12; jurist.

Marcus Rustius Rufinus. 212-17; former *speculatore*.

Marcus Opellius Macrinus. 212-17; became emperor after killing Caracalla.

Ulpius Julianus. ?-218; killed in Syria while helping Macrinus.

P. Valerius Comazon. Appointed by Elagabalus in 218; retired by 222.

Julius Flavianus. Elagabalus's prefect in 218; reappointed by Alexander Severus in 222.

Geminius Chrestus. 222-?; killed at instigation of Mamaea.

Antiochianis. Killed while trying to save Elagabalus.

Domitius Ulpianus. Famous jurist; banished by Elagabalus, then reinstated by Alexander. Killed in 228.

Julius Paulus. Appointed about 225; executed in 235 by Maximinus.

M. Attius Carnelianus. 230-35; executed by Maximinus.

M. Aedinus Julianus. 223-38; killed with Maximinus at Aquelia.

144

P. Aelius Vitalianus. Maximinus's commander in Rome; killed in 238.

Pinarius Valens. Killed in 238 with emperors Maximus and Balbinus.

Domitius. 238-42; organized the revolt against Maximus and Balbinus.

C. Julius Priscus. 241-?; brother of Emperor Philip.

Furius Sabinus Aquila Timesithius. 241-43; father-in-law of the emperor Alexander Severus.

Maecius Gordianus. ?-244; relative of the emperor Gordian III.

Marcus Julius Philippus. Appointed in 243 by Gordian III.

Ballista. 260-61; field commander for Valerian in Persia.

*Mulvius Gallicanus. Guard commander for the city of Rome under Valerian, 254-57.

*Ablavius Murena. 254-57; shared command with Gallicanus.

*Baebius Macer. 258; in Byzantium with Valerian.

Successianus. 257; captured by Persians with Valerian.

L. Petronius Taurus Volusianus. About 260-67.

Aurelius Heraclianus. 267-68; was involved in plot to kill Gallienus.

Julius Placidianus. 271-73; served as consul with Aurelian.

Moesius Gallicanus. In 275, arranged guard approval of Tacitus.

Florian. Half-brother of Tacitus; made prefect in 275.

*Capito. 275-82; served both Tacitus and Probus.

Marcus Aurelius Carus. After 276 to 282; became emperor after Probus.

Tiberius Claudius Aurelius Aristobulis. 282-84; prefect for Carus, Carinus, and Diocletian.

M. Florius Aper. 283-84; killed personally by Diocletian.

Africanus Hannibalianus. 295-96; city prefect in 297.

Julius Asclepiodotus. 285-97; commanded invasion of Britain in 296.

Anulinus. Led revolt in 306 against Severus; put Maxentius in power; may have commanded guard at the Milvian Bridge.

Emperors Serving With Legions

Vespasian	commanded II Augusta in 43
Titus	had command of at least one legion during the Jerusalem campaign
Trajan	commanded VII Gemina in 89 in northern Spain
Hadrian	commanded I Minervia in Dacia about 106 and had previously been a military tribune with II Adiutrix and V Macedonica
Pertinax	commanded I Adiutrix and had previous service as a military tribune
Didius Julianus	commanded XXII Primigenia in Germany
Septimus Severus	commanded IV Scythica in Massiam (probably Masyaf in western Syria)
Maximinus	prefect of II Traiana in 232 in Nicopolis, Egypt
Aurelian	commanded X Gemina
Probus	commanded X Gemina

Stations of the Legions

Localities listed below are those where legions were based for one or more years. Temporary stations and sites of battles are not included. The Roman name is shown in parentheses when appropriate. A Roman name with an asterisk indicates that the base was in the vicinity of the named city or town but not necessarily at precisely the same place. Letters and numbers following a Roman name indicate approximate direction and distance in miles from the present town or city.

BRITAIN

Caerleon	II Augusta
Chester (Deva)	II Adiutrix
	XX Valeria Victrix
Gloucester (Glevum)	II Augusta
	XX Valeria Victrix
Lincoln (Lindum)	II Adiutrix
	IX Hispana
Newcastle	VI Victrix
Wroxeter (Viroconium)	XX Valeria Victrix
York (Eburicum)	VI Victrix
	IX Hispana

FRANCE

Lyon (Lugdunum)	I Italica
Strasbourg (Argentorate)	II Augusta
	VII Augusta
	XXI Rapax

SPAIN

Leon	VII Gemina

147

NETHERLANDS

Nijmegen (Noviomagnus*)   IX   Hispana
    X   Gemina
    XXII   Primigenia

GERMANY

Bonn (Bonno)   I   Minervia
    XV   Primegenia
    XXI   Rapax

Cologne (Colonia
Agrippina)   I   Germanica
    V   Alaudae
    XX   Valeria Victrix
    XXI   Rapax

Mainz (Mogantiacum)   I   Adiutrix
    IV   Macedonica
    XIV   Gemina
    XV   Primigenia
    XVI   Gallica
    XXI   Rapax
    XXII   Primigenia

Neuss (Novaesium)   VI   Victrix
    XVI   Gallica
    XX   Valeria Victrix

Regensburg (Castra
Regina)   II   Italica
    III   Italica

Trier   I   Germanica
Xanten (Vetera)   VI   Victrix
    V   Alaudae
    XXI   Rapax
    XXII   Primigenia
    XXX   Ulpia

SWITZERLAND

Windisch (Vindonissa)   XI   Claudia
    XIII   Gemina
    XXI   Rapax

148

ITALY

Albano	II	Parthica
Aquileia	XI	Claudia
Trieste(Emona* NE50)	XV	Apollinaris

AUSTRIA

Linz (Lauriacum*)	II	Italica
Vienna (Vindobonna)	X	Gemina
	XIII	Gemina
	XV	Apollinaris
Hainburg (Carnuntum*)	VII	Gemina
	XII	Fulminata
	XIV	Gemina
	XV	Apollinaris

HUNGARY

Budapest (Aquincum*)	II	Adiutrix
Komeron (Brigetio*)	I	Adiutrix

CZECHOSLOVAKIA

Trencin*	II	Adiutrix

YUGOSLAVIA

Belgrade (Singidunum)	II	Adiutrix
	IV	Flavia firma
Knin (Burnum)	IV	Flavia firma
	XI	Claudia
Pozarevac (Viminacium*)	IV	Flavia
	VII	Claudia
Marburg (Poetovio)	XIII	Gemina
Zagreb (Siscia*)	IX	Hispana

RUMANIA

Alba Iulia (Apulum*)	XIII	Gemina
Baila (Troesmis*)	V	Macedonica

Balta (Mehadia*)	XIII	Gemina
Cluj-Napoca (Potaissa*)	V	Macedonica
Vulcan, Transylvania		
(Sarmizegethusa NW*)	XXX	Ulpia

BULGARIA

Archar (Ratiaria*)	XIII	Gemina
Knizha (Oescus*)	V	Macedonica
Silistria (Durostorum)	XI	Claudia
Svishtov (Novae)	I	Italica

TURKEY

Antioch	IV	Scythica
(Cyrrhus)	IV	Scythica
	X	Fretensis
Birecik (Zeugma*)	IV	Scythica
Erzinkin (Satala* N20)	XV	Apollinaris
	XVI	Flavia firma
Malatya (Melitene)	V	Macedonica
	XII	Fulminata
Samsat (Samosata)	VI	Ferrata
	XVI	Flavia firma

SYRIA

Al Mausil (Singara*		
SW30)	I	Parthica
	III	Parthica
Al Qamishli (Nisibis*)	I	Parthica
	III	Parthica
Damascus (Danabe* NE)	III	Gallica
Latakia (Laodicia)	VI	Ferrata
Tarsus (Raphanaea* E30)	III	Gallica

ISRAEL

| Jerusalem | X | Fretensis |

JORDAN

Irbid (Bostra*)   VI   Ferrata
                              III   Cyrenaica

EGYPT

Alexandria   II   Traiana
                              III   Cyrenaica
                                V   Macedonica
                               XV   Apollinaris
                             XXII   Deiotariana
Luxor (Coptos* N)   III   Cyrenaica

ALGERIA

Batna (Lambaesis*)   III   Augusta
Tebessa (Ammaedara*
    NE20)   III   Augusta

Lifelines of the Legions

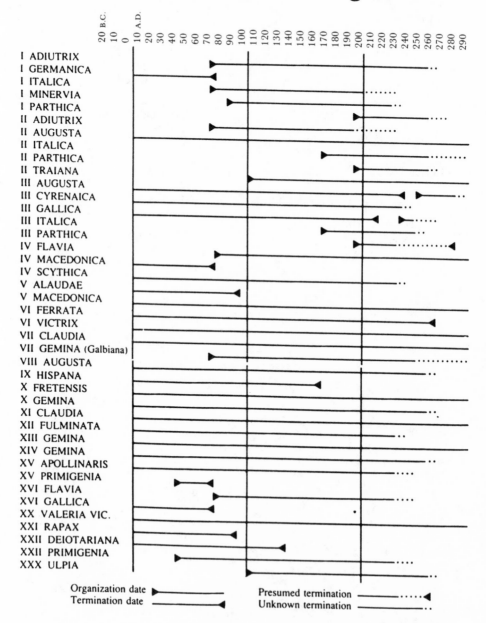

Bibliography

Classical sources:

Dio, Cassius. *Roman History*. Translated by Earnest Cary. Cambridge, Mass.: Harvard University Press, 1924. Nine volumes. Volumes seven and eight include Dio's books 56-70 and cover the first 138 years of our era. The detailed descriptions of battle and the conduct of troops are valuable. These volumes also offer amusing and somewhat salacious descriptions of the private lives of the emperors and their ladies.

Herodian. *The History*. Translated by C.R. Whittaker. Loeb Classical Library. New York: Penguin Books, 1969. Two volumes. Herodian rarely mentions a legion by name, but the extensive footnotes provide valuable indentifications.

Josephus. *The Jewish War*. Translated by G.A. Williamson. New York: Penguin Books, 1959. This book is precise history and contains descriptions of the organization and conduct of the legions. Three maps.

Lewis, Naphtali and Reinhold, Meyer. *Roman Civilization Sourcebook II: The Empire*. Harper, Torchbook edition, 1966, New York. This volume, with introduction and notes and a superb bibliography, is valuable in its presentation in translation of a number of historic documents pertaining to the praetorians and their prefects. The index is most helpful.

Lives of the Later Caesars. Translated by Anthony Birley. New York: Penguin Books, 1976. The first part of the *Augustan History*. This volume is skillfully edited, with entertaining footnotes. An excellent index lists legions.

Plutarch. *The Lives of the Noble Grecians and Romans*. Translated by John Dryden, with revisions by Arthur Hugh Clough. New York: Modern Library, n.d. Offers extensive biographies of Galba and Otho.

Scriptores Historiae Augustae. Loeb Classical Library. Cambridge, Mass.: Harvard University Press, 1922. Three volumes. These volumes are entertaining but filled with misinformation. Excellent notes and index.

Suetonius. *The Twelve Caesars.* Translated by Robert Graves. New York: Penguin Books, 1957.

Tacitus. *The Agricola and the Germania.* Translated by H. Mattingly and S.A. Handford. New York: Penguin Books, 1970. This volume gives a detailed account of the battle at Mons Graupius.

----------. *The Annals of Imperial Rome.* Translated by Michael Grant. New York: Penguin Books, 1956. Legion facts are hidden among stories of the emperors.

----------. *The Histories.* Translated by Kenneth Wellesley. New York: Penguin Books, 1975.

Modern sources:

Birley, Anthony. *Life in Roman Britain.* London: Batsford Ltd., 1976. This book has a good chapter on the Roman army in Britain, with a useful map. The index is helpful in dealing with seven legions.

Blair, Peter Hunter. *Roman Britain and Early England, 55 B.C.-A.D. 871.* New York: Norton, 1963.

Bowder, Diana, ed. *Who Was Who in the Roman World, 753 B.C.-476 A.D.* Ithaca, N.Y.: Cornell University Press, 1980.

Breeze, David J., and Dobson, Brian. *Hadrian's Wall.* New York: Penguin Books, 1978. This is an exceptionally fine study, well researched and clearly presented. There is much information on the Roman army in Britain not found elsewhere. The index has numerous legion listings.

Burn, A.R. *The Romans in Britain: An Anthology of Inscriptions.* Columbia, S.C.: University of South Carolina Press, 1967.

Cook, S.A., Adcock, F.E., and Charlesworth, M.P. eds. *Cambridge Ancient History.* Volumes 10-12. Cambridge: Cambridge University Press, 1939. These three volumes are without a doubt the most useful studies of the Roman Empire, the Roman army, and the praetorian guard for the period 44 B.C. to A.D. 325. There are numerous maps, and each volume has a superb index.

Durant, Will. *Caesar and Christ*. New York: Simon and Schuster, 1944.

Durry, Marcel. *Les Cohortes Prétoriennes*. Paris: Bibliothèque Des Écoles Françaises D'Athênes et de Rome, 1938. A general paper on the praetorians. It contains an interesting discussion of the structure of the castra and a description of the battle of the Milvian Bridge.

Encyclopaedia Britannica. Cambridge University Press, 1911-1912. This world famous eleventh edition is studded with classical data not readily available elsewhere. There is an unsigned article in Volume XXII, pages 245-246 that gives a good general account of the praetorians.

Grant, Michael. *The Climax of Rome*. Cardinal edition, Sphere Books, Ltd., London, 1974. Although there are few mentions of the praetorians, this is excellent background for understanding third-century Rome.

Headley, John. *The Conflict between Nobles and Magistrates, in the Franche-Comté, 1508-1518*. Journal of Medieval and Renaissance Studies, Durham, N.C.: Duke University Press, Spring 1979. The appendix contains an informative discussion of the ambivalent position of the praetorian prefect as military commander, chief justice, and head of the imperial administration.

Howe, Laurence Lee. *Praetorian Prefects from Commodus to Diocletian*. Chicago: University of Chicago Press, 1942. This discussion of the praetorian prefect is unfortunately out of print. Appendix I has invaluable accounts of the lives of the prefects from A.D. 180 until the time of Diocletian.

Luttwak, Edward N. *The Grand Strategy of the Roman Empire from the First Century A.D. to the Third*. Baltimore: Johns Hopkins University Press, 1976. This book provides an interesting discussion of the strategic problem and makes a number of references to the praetorians and individual legions. There are fifteen maps.

MacMullen, Ramsay. *Roman Governments' Response to Crisis A.D. 235-337*. New Haven: Yale University Press, 1976. Despite little interest in or liking for the praetorians, the author gives one chapter on the defense of the empire that is well worth reading.

----------. *Soldier and Civilian in the Later Roman Empire.* Cambridge, Mass.: Harvard University Press, 1963. There are several references to praetorian prefects and the administration of the later empire.

Mellersh, H.D.L. *The Roman Soldier.* New York: Taplinger Publishing Co., 1965. This text provides general background.

Parker, H.M.D. *The Roman Legions.* New York: Barnes & Noble, 1958. This is a very thorough, if rather contentious, study of the legions up to the year 180. Appendix A is a unique and valuable report on the origins and nomenclature of the Augustan legions. An excellent index provides easy references to individual legions.

Perowne, Stewart. *Hadrian.* London: Hodden and Stoughton, 1960. An entertaining biography. It has numerous mentions of the praetorians.

Richmond, I.A. *Roman Britain.* Baltimore: Penguin Books, 1963. The first sixty-five pages present a good military history of the Roman occupation with six maps. The index lists legions individually.

Scullard, H. H. *Roman Britain, Outpost of the Empire.* London: Thomas and Hudson, 1979. This does not address itself specifically to legions, nor does the index make any reference to them. There are, however, some useful data on legionary fortresses and on the diet and life of the Roman soldier in Britain.

Webster, Graham. *The Roman Imperial Army of the First and Second Centuries* A.D. New York: Funk and Wagnalls, 1969. This is one of the most useful and thoroughly researched books on the Roman army. It covers the army in the field and in peacetime activities. There are good maps and charts and a superb index that follows individual legions by name from station to station.

Wellesley, Kenneth. *The Long Year* A.D. *69.* Boulder, Colo.: Westview Press, 1976. This history contains interpretations of the first and second battles of Cremona with several charts and maps.

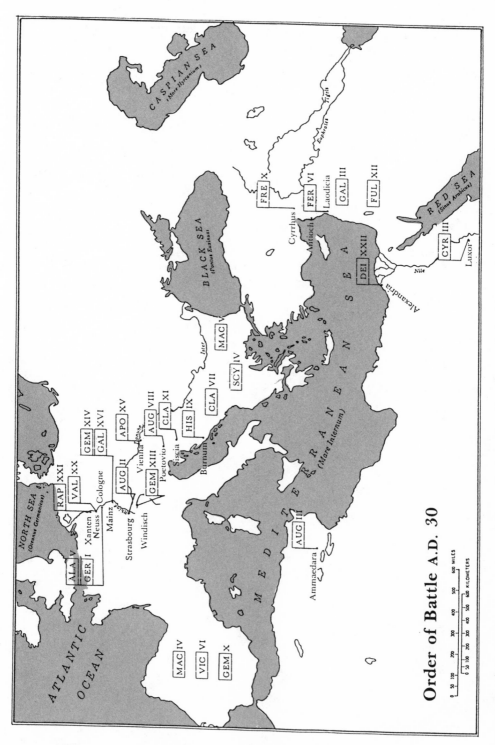

Order of Battle A.D. 30

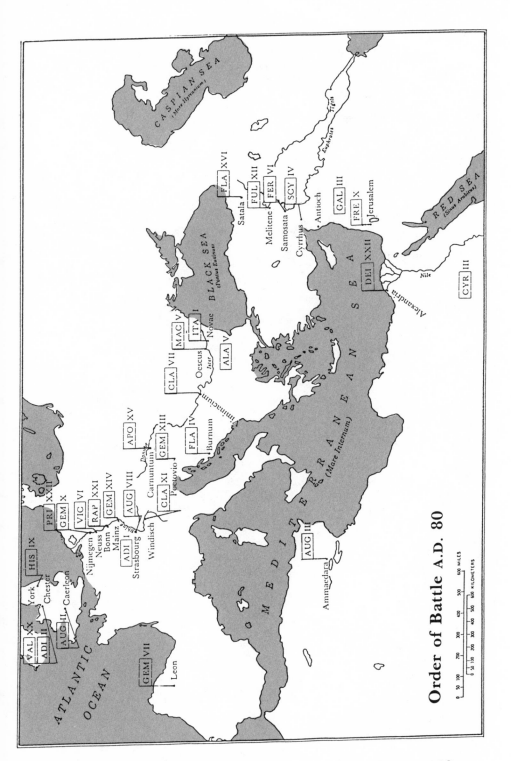

Order of Battle A.D. 80

159

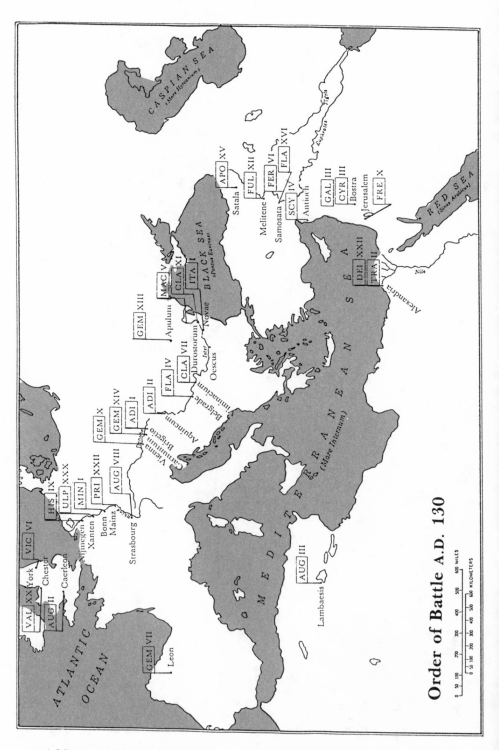

Order of Battle A.D. 130

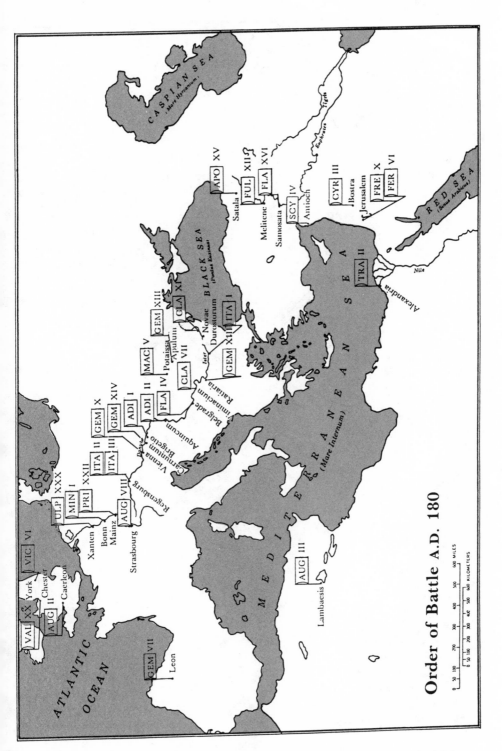

Order of Battle A.D. 180

161

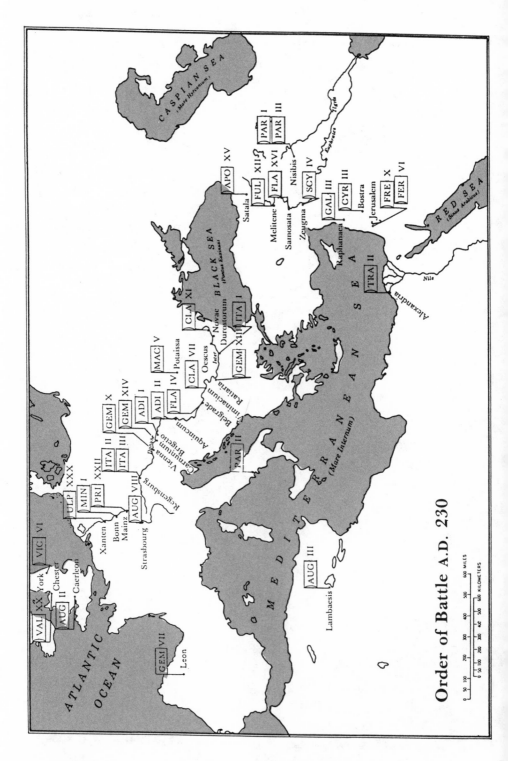

Order of Battle A.D. 230

---

* Italicized page number indicates illustration in text

Dacian wars, 113, 119, 122, 123, 125, 127-8
Dalmatia, 10, 22, 43, 111, 112, 123
Danaba, 102
Danube, 1, 27, 39, 40, 44, 46, 53, 54, 59, 60, 61, 79, 81, 82, 84, 88, 92, 94, 95, 96, 100, 105, 106, 110, 111, 112,113, 114, 119, 120, 121, 122, 123, 124, 125, 126, 127, 128
Dead Sea, 97, 98, 103
death, Roman way of, 22-27
Decebalus, 35, 36, 123, 126
decimation, 78
Decius, Caius Messius Quintus, 58, 59, 60
Deiotarus, 115
Delta, 95
Densus, Sempronius, 20, 84, 134
Dio, 11, 26
Diocletian, D. Aurelius, 24, 64, 65, 80, 94,*112*, 113, 127, 132
Dobruja, 59
Domitian, Titus Flavius, 31, 32, 33, 34, 74, 79, 85, 110, 112, 114, *115*, 116, *117*, 120, 121, 123, 124, 125, 126, 127, 131
Domitius (prefect), 57
door ceremony, 33
Drava river, 111
Drusus, son of Tiberius, 6-7, 9, 10, *88*, 89
Drusus, son of Germanicus, 10
Dumbarton, Rock of, 83
Durostorum (Silistra), 112
Dusseldorf, 114

E

Edessa, 131
Egypt, 17, 34, 81, 96, 108, 109, 115, 127
Elagabalus (nee Varius Avitus Bassianus), 48, 49, 50, 51, *99*, 101, 102, 124, 130
Elbe, 7
Emesa, 109
Emmaus, 93
Emona, 95
emperors, Roman
  from 26 B.C. to A.D. 312, 141
  who served with legions, 146
Ems river, 8
English Channel, 13
Ethiopia, 17, 118
Euphrates river, 36, 52, 57, 81, 92, 95, 97, 99, 101, 103, 105, 109, 110, 123, 133

F

Fadilla, 41
Fano, 63
Firmus, Plotius, 21
Fiume, 89
Flavia firma, 114
Flavianus, Julius, 52
Florianus, Publius, 43
fleet, Roman, 1, 103, 120
Fortunatus, Petronius, 104
Fortuna Primigenia, *116*, 117
France, 7, 79, 107, 119
Franks, 125
fretensis, 96
Frisians, 110
Fuscus, Cornelius, 34, 36

G

Gaius, 116
Galatia, 115
Galba, Servius Sulpicius, 19, 20, 78, 79, 84, *109*, 117, 119, 120, 121
Galerius, 66, 94
Galilee, 95
Gallicanus, Moesius, 62, 63
Gallicanus, Mulvius 61
Gallienus, Publius Licinius, 60, 61, 79, *111*, 121, 129, 131, 133
Gallus, C. Cestus, 104
Gallus, Caius Vibius Trebonianus, 24, 59, 60
Gamala, 93, 96, 97
Gamara 92, 95
Gaul, 12, 13, 21, 44, 47, 66, 79, 88, 99, 100, 114, 130
  revolt in, 19
Genialis, T. Flavius, 44, 45
Germanicus, 7, 8, 9, 16, 25, 97, *106*
Germany, 19, 43, 53, 54, 84, 85, 104, 106, 110, 112, 113, 114, 115, 117, 118, 120, 122, 128, 129
  campaign in, 7-8
  rebellion in, 21-22
Geta, Lucius, 15
Geta, Publius Septimius, 46
Gibraltar, 64
Gloucester, 83, 87, 107
Gordian I (Marcus Antonius Gordianus Sempronianus Romanus), 24, 54, 108, 127, *130*, 131
Gordian II, 54, 108
Gordian III, 33, 54, 56, 57, 58, 77, 108
Gordianus, Maecius, 58

Gracian, 88
Greece, 18, 38, 81
Gulf of Venice, 4, 55, 130

H

Hadrian, Publius Aelius, 23, 36, 37, 38,
    77, 78, 82, 85, 98, *108*, 122, 124,
    125
    attributes of, 125
Hadrian's Wall, *76*, 80, 82, 85, 107
Han Empire, 102
Hannibalianus, Africanus, 64
Hellespont, 57
Heraclianus, Aurelius, 61
Herodian, 56
High Priests monument, 96
Holland, 90
Honorius, 82, 86, 88
Hostilianus, 59
Hungary, 81, 88, 90, 112

I

Iceni, 89
Illyricum (Yugoslavia), 10, 86
Irbid, 109
Israel, 81
Italy, 28, 129, 130

J

Janus, temple of, 33
Japha, 92
Jerusalem, 11, 81, 91, 93, 94, 96, 97, 98,
    103, 104, 127
John the Baptist, 97
Jordan, 97, 103, 104, 108
Jordan river, 97
Josephus, 91, 92, 95
Jotapata, 92, 93, 95
Judea, 95, 98, 103
Julianus, 31
Julianus, M. Aedinus, 53, 55
Julianus, Didius, 43, 118
Julianus, L. Julius Vehilius Grafus, 41
Julianus, Salvius, 39
Julianus, Ulpius, 48
Jupiter, temple of, 31
Justus, Cantonius, 14, 15

K

Kent, 89
Knin, 112, 123
Komaron, 121
Kostolacz, 111

L

Laco, Cornelius, 19, 20
Laco, Publius Graecinius, 11
Laetus, A. Maecius, 45
Laetus, Quintus Aemilus, 40, 41, 42
Lambaesis, 54, 77, 108
Laodici, 102
Lascivius, Triarius Maternus, 42
Lauriacum, 128
Lebanon, 81
legionnaires
    engineering achievements of, 76-77
    uniform and equipment of, 3
    wages of, 1-2, 74
legions, Roman
    discipline in, 78
    lifelines of, 152
    officer exchange among, 104
    organization and efficiency of, 73-81,
        132-34
    stations of, 147-51
    uniformity of, 77
    I Adiutrix, 78, 104, 115, 134
        history of, 120-22
    I Germanicus, 7, 28, 117
        history of, 106-07
    I Italica, 104
        history of, 118-19
    I Minervia, 85, 104
        history of, 124-25
    I Parthica, 131
        history of, 129-30
    II Adiutrix, 30, 82
        history of, 122
    II Augusta, 7, 74, 76, 77, 79, 82, 85,
        87, 89, 104, 134
        history of, 107
    II Italica Pia, 134
        history of, 128-29
    II Parthica, 1, 46, 47, 48, 55, 104, 127,
        129, 134
        history of, 130-31
    II Triana, 99
        history of, 126-27
    III Augusta, 76, 77, 89, 104
        history of, 108
    III Cyrenaica, 104, 108, 115

M

169

T

U

V

W

X Y Z

COLONEL ROBERT E. EVANS was educated at Middlesex School, Le Rosey in Switzerland, and Harvard. At various times in his lively career he has been a newspaper editor, a book publisher, and a public affairs officer for the U.S. Department of State. After service in World War II, he returned to the Army in 1947 and over the next 18 years was on active duty in Germany, Vietnam, and Hawaii. He retired in 1965 and has since devoted himself to civic affairs in Washington. He is a vice president of the English-Speaking Union of the United States.

What Makes Me

AMISH?

Charles George

KIDHAVEN PRESS
An imprint of Thomson Gale, a part of The Thomson Corporation

THOMSON
™
GALE

Detroit • New York • San Francisco • San Diego • New Haven, Conn.
Waterville, Maine • London • Munich

LIBRARY OF CONGRESS CATALOGING-IN-PUBLICATION DATA

George, Charles, 1949–
  Amish / by Charles George.
    p. cm. — (What makes me a— ?)
  Includes bibliographical references and index.
  ISBN 0-7377-3081-1 (hardcover : alk. paper)
  1. Amish—Juvenile literature. I. Title. II. Series.
  BX8129.A5G46 2005
  289.7'3—dc22

                                        2005010916

Printed in the United States of America

CONTENTS

Simple Folk, Simple Faith

Approximately 180,000 Amish people live in the United States, as either members of the more traditional Old Order Amish or of less **conservative** groups. Recently, thanks to movies, television shows, and advertisements, the Amish have become more familiar to Americans. Images of these simple folks living uncomplicated lives, separated from the modern world, draw envy from people living in a world of terrorist threats, traffic jams, and cell phones. Who are the Amish? Why do they separate themselves from modern society? How do they live with so few modern conveniences?

The Amish are conservative Christians, tracing their origins to Anabaptists, religious reformers in Europe who broke from the Catholic Church and early Protestant reformers due to differences in beliefs and practices. Though they share many beliefs, ceremonies, and

An elderly Amish couple rides along a Kentucky street in their horse-drawn buggy.

holidays with other Christians, the Amish interpret the words of the *Bible*, their most sacred text, quite literally.

Unlike many churches, the Amish have no national organization. Each local church stands alone. Its elders educate youth on Amish ideals. Through this close-knit structure, the Amish have been able to maintain their simple lifestyle and encourage the order and discipline necessary to continue unchanged in an ever-changing world.

CHAPTER ONE

How Did the Amish Religion Begin?

T he Amish consider themselves neither Protestant nor Catholic. They believe their church is a separate branch of Christianity. Their roots go back to 16th century Europe, to the beginnings of the Protestant Reformation.

By the 16th century, the Catholic Church had grown from a small religious **sect** to a powerful economic and political force in Europe. Christians dominated European society. Governments required citizens to **baptize** children shortly after they were born. The Church held considerable wealth, including vast tracts of land. With wealth and power came corruption.

Protestant Reformation

By 1517, some Christians, particularly in northern Europe, believed the Catholic Church had lost sight of its original mission and had become corrupt. They believed the Church had become too powerful, with priests and bishops misusing that power. In that year, Martin Luther, a Catholic priest, posted 95 grievances against the Catholic Church on the door of the Wittenberg, Germany, church. His protest began the Protestant Reformation and eventually led to the establishment of various Protestant denominations.

Among Luther's views was the idea that each individual could receive forgiveness and entry into heaven by faith alone. Ceremonies performed by a priest or a pope were not necessary. He believed each person

In 1517, Martin Luther began a movement against the Catholic Church that became known as the Protestant Reformation.

than the Catholic Church. He became a leader in the Anabaptist movement. Dutch, Swiss, and German Anabaptists eventually became known as Mennonites. Menno's writings are found in many Mennonite and Amish homes today.

Over the next 150 years, differences arose between Anabaptists in Switzerland and those in other countries, where persecution was less severe. In some areas, followers feared their members had made too many compromises with the society around them.

Jacob Amman

One Anabaptist elder critical of his church's practices was Jacob Amman, from France. He criticized the fact that church members commemorated the Lord's Supper only once a year. He wondered why they did not practice foot washing as a symbol of humility and service, as Christ had done during the Last Supper. He also questioned whether non-Anabaptists who had lived good lives would be allowed to enter heaven.

Amman believed his church should practice Meidung, the **shunning** of people who have been **banned**. Banning is forbidding someone

In 1536, Menno Simons left the Catholic Church and became an Anabaptist.

10

from participating in church services. It is used when someone has sinned and has not been willing to admit the sin and ask for forgiveness. Shunning is socially avoiding a person, pretending they do not exist, as a form of punishment. A person who is shunned is not looked at, spoken to, or spoken about by anyone in his or her community. Such isolation is difficult to bear and usually brings repentance.

In 1693, Amman and others traveled to Switzerland to find out how Anabaptists there felt about these issues. When local church leaders refused to give him quick answers, he banned, or **excommunicated**, them. Most Swiss congregations disagreed with Amman, but many in Alsace agreed with him. Those who followed him became Amish. Those who did not remained Mennonite.

Seven years later, in 1700, the Amish tried to reconcile with the Mennonites. Amman and others admitted they had been too harsh, but refused to give up their demand for Meidung. The reconciliation failed, and Mennonites and Amish have remained separate since. Today, most Amish know little about Jacob Amman. They consider themselves Anabaptists, whose roots go back to that first adult baptism in Zurich, Switzerland, in 1525.

To America

In the 1700s, the Amish in Europe faced persecution, oppression, various local wars, and famine. The newly settled colonies of North America offered a new start.

Where the Amish Religion Began

In 1517, Martin Luther posts grievances against the Catholic Church on a church door in Germany, starting the Protestant Reformation.

Martin Luther

London

Berlin

In 1525, Anabaptists meet in Switzerland to perform the first adult baptism.

In 1536, Menno Simons leaves the Catholic Church in Holland to join the Anabaptists. He becomes a leader in the movement.

EUROPE

In 1693, the Anabaptists meet in Switzerland and disagree over Meidung and other issues. They split into two groups, the Mennonites and the Amish.

Rome

No one knows exactly when the first Amish settlers reached the New World, since the Amish keep no organized church records. However, they followed Mennonite immigrants who arrived as early as 1663.

Most Amish settled in Pennsylvania, west of present-day Philadelphia. There, they faced frontier hardships, depending upon each other for survival. Pressure from other church groups trying to lure the Amish to their churches forced many to move farther west, into Ohio, Indiana, Illinois, Iowa, and Ontario, Canada.

A Further Split

During the 1800s, more Amish came to the United States and Canada. When they arrived, they found those who had come earlier to be stricter in their interpretation of the *Bible* and in their practices. Not willing to **conform**, many new arrivals moved farther west. By the mid-1860s, America's Amish were divided. Some were quite conservative, while others wanted flexibility in their dress, way of life, and religion.

In 1862, members of Amish congregations across the country met in Wayne County, Ohio, to decide how they would proceed. This meeting did little to iron out differences. In 1865, conservative Amish delegates issued an ultimatum—either turn your backs on the worldly practices of the progressives and be welcomed back into the fellowship as "brothers and sisters" or leave.

The result was another split in the Amish Church. The progressive majority came to be called Amish

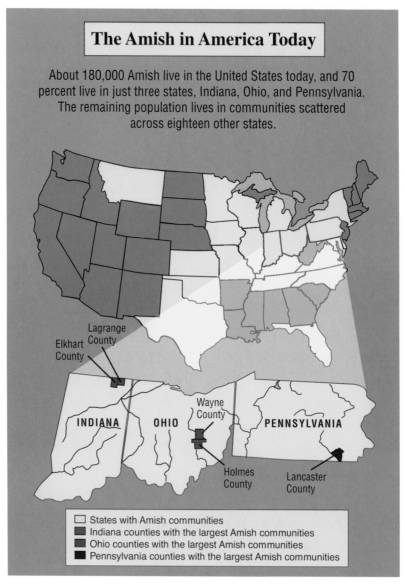

The Amish in America Today

About 180,000 Amish live in the United States today, and 70 percent live in just three states, Indiana, Ohio, and Pennsylvania. The remaining population lives in communities scattered across eighteen other states.

Lagrange County
Elkhart County

Wayne County

INDIANA   OHIO   PENNSYLVANIA

Holmes County
Lancaster County

☐ States with Amish communities
■ Indiana counties with the largest Amish communities
■ Ohio counties with the largest Amish communities
■ Pennsylvania counties with the largest Amish communities

Mennonites. Conservatives—those who favored the old ways—were eventually called Old Order Amish. Old Order Amish support strict obedience to a list of rules called the Ordnung, or Order, which tells them how to dress, behave, and practice their religion.

CHAPTER TWO

What Do I Believe?

What make the Amish unique in today's hectic world are not their religious beliefs. They share core beliefs with Christians around the world, both Catholic and Protestant. What separates them is how they incorporate those beliefs into everyday life.

Shared Beliefs

Like other Christians, the Amish believe Jesus was the Son of God, and that he took human form to teach humanity how to live. They also believe he died on the cross and was resurrected, returning to heaven to live eternally as part of the Holy Trinity—God the Father, Jesus, and the Holy Spirit.

The Amish consider the *Holy Bible* their most sacred text, their source of religious principles. They believe its writers were inspired by God, that the *Bible* is without error, and that its words should be interpreted literally.

God holds the crucified Jesus in this painting. The Amish, like all Christians, believe that Jesus is the son of God.

The Amish believe in heaven and hell and that Satan exists. They believe each human has an eternal soul and that to avoid eternity in hell, a person must choose to be baptized as an adult into the Amish Church. Like many Christian groups, the Amish believe theirs is the only true church. Only people who have been baptized Amish have a chance at going to heaven.

They believe the church is the body of Christ on Earth. To follow God's teaching, one must submit to the authority of the church. Because they believe their church has been given the authority to interpret the will of God, submitting to the church is submitting to God.

Beliefs Unique to the Amish

Several practices set the Amish apart from other Christian denominations. One is their insistence on remaining separate from the world. They believe the *Bible* clearly states why separation from worldly things is necessary.

Romans 12:2 says, "And do not be conformed to this world, but be transformed by the renewing of your mind, that you may prove what is that good and acceptable and perfect will of God." Second Corinthians 6:17 states, "Therefore come out from among them, and be separate, says the Lord." First John 2:15 says, "Do not love the world or the things in the world. If anyone loves the world, the love of the Father is not in him."

The Amish also practice nonviolence. They refuse to participate in military service, they do not fight back when attacked, and they forgive those who mistreat them. To be nonviolent is to be "in" the world without being "of" the world. Central to their faith is the desire to live at peace with one another. Most Christians recall the words of Jesus in Luke 6:29: "To him who strikes you on the one cheek, offer the other also." Christ's message in the Sermon on the Mount was to be nonviolent. All true Christians are supposed to practice nonviolence, but few do it better than the Amish.

An Amish man in Pennsylvania holds up his copy of the *Bible* during a worship service.

Christian churches believe baptism is necessary for **salvation**. The Amish, unlike some Protestant denominations, believe only adult baptism is valid. They believe a person must be old enough to make a conscious decision to be baptized. To them, baptism and the associated vows are significant steps not to be taken lightly.

Unlike some other Christian groups, however, the Amish do not believe baptism is a guaranteed ticket to heaven. They believe a person must live a life dedicated to the service of God and that good works—charity, faith, obedience to the church, and humility—are necessary before God grants a person salvation. For guidance, the Amish look to the *Bible* and to other documents from their past.

Amish Articles of Faith

In addition to the *Holy Bible*, the Amish consider two other documents important guidelines in their lives—the Schleitheim Articles of 1527 and the Dordrecht Confession of Faith of 1632. The first document came out of a 1527 meeting of Swiss and German Anabaptists known as the Swiss Brethren. They met secretly in Schleitheim, a small village in Switzerland, to formalize their beliefs. They compiled a list of seven core beliefs called the Brotherly Agreement, later referred to as the Schleitheim Articles.

Amish Mennonite volunteers from Pennsylvania build a fence to help people in Montana who lost their homes in a 2003 fire.

Briefly, these stated that only adult baptisms were valid, church members who sinned but refused to confess and repent were banned from the church, and only baptized church members could take part in the religious ceremony called **communion**, the Lord's Supper. The articles also declared that Christians should separate themselves from the evils of the world, be nonviolent, not participate in politics, and not swear oaths.

About a century later, in 1632, a group of Mennonites in Holland amended that list of principles with the Dordrecht Confession of Faith. The authors of this document prescribed not only banning for church members guilty of unrepented sins, but also shunning. It also called for church members to begin the practice of foot washing during the communion ceremony and reemphasized the importance of strict separation from the world.

The Ordnung

A fourth code of behavior, based on **scripture**, governs the lifestyle, appearance, and actions of the Amish. It has never been written down. It is an oral tradition passed down within Amish communities—the Ordnung. By becoming baptized into the Amish Church, young Amish people promise to serve God. To do this the Amish way requires obedience to the Ordnung, and these unwritten rules cover a variety of issues.

For example, only bottled propane or natural gas is allowed to operate farm equipment and modern appliances such as stoves and refrigerators. Electricity is forbidden. TVs, computers, and radios are forbidden

Amish men, wearing traditional black clothing and broad-brimmed hats, stand outside a Pennsylvania store.

because using them would expose the Amish to the corruption of the outside world. Owning motorized vehicles is also forbidden. They might encourage people to travel too far away from home, possibly breaking up tightly knit communities.

Most Christian denominations emphasize personal success and individuality. The Ordnung emphasizes conformity. Individual differences might lead to pride. Pride leads to jealousy and envy. The simple Amish style of dress is the most visible example of this.

Men wear plain black clothing with suspenders and broad-brimmed black hats. Belts are forbidden. Belt buckles are considered a form of jewelry that might lead to pride. Buttons are not allowed to fasten Amish

Wearing traditional dresses, bonnets, and aprons, Amish women prepare chicken dinners at a country fair in Montana.

clothing, because they are considered worldly. Instead, clothes are fastened with hooks and eyes or with straight pins.

The Ordnung requires women to wear plain, solid-colored dresses, bonnets, and aprons. Patterns might instill pride. Amish women do not wear jewelry. In 1 Timothy 2:9, Paul instructed that "women adorn themselves in modest apparel, with propriety and moderation, not with braided hair or gold or pearls or costly clothing."

Amish women wear small white head coverings at all times, because a verse in 1 Corinthians says women must have their heads covered when praying, and they never know when they might pray. For the Amish, praying and other religious activities are not reserved only for Sunday worship services. They live their beliefs every day of their lives.

CHAPTER THREE

How Do I Practice My Faith?

I t might surprise outsiders who think the Amish are extremely religious to know they hold Sunday worship services only every other week. Also, the Amish do not have church buildings or a national church organization. The Amish do not have church choirs or use musical instruments. Their ministers are not professionally trained and do not prepare sermons prior to religious services, but each church is organized according to strict Ordnung guidelines.

Church Organization

Each Amish congregation is independent and has its own leadership. The Amish do not allow women to serve in positions of authority. Those are reserved for men. Each church has a *Völliger Diener*, translated as "full servant" or bishop, who provides spiritual leadership, preaches, and performs baptisms, weddings, and

Because women are forbidden from serving in positions of authority, only Amish men can hold church positions.

funerals. He is usually the oldest ordained man in the congregation.

Most congregations choose two men to serve as *Diener zum Buch*, translated as "servant of the book," or minister. These men assist in preaching and teaching. Each congregation has several men who serve as *Armendiener*, or deacons. During services, they read aloud from the *Bible* and help in various ways, including administering the church's fund for the poor.

When it is time to fill a position of authority, usually when a church official dies, the Amish conduct an **ordination**. After two weeks of prayer and contemplation, everyone is allowed to nominate someone for the lifelong position. Men who want the job cannot say so, however, because they would be accused of pride and be disqualified.

Those nominated by the most people draw lots to see who is chosen. This way, the Amish believe God participates in the selection. Being ordained is considered a burden rather than an honor. Those chosen must exhibit the highest moral standards, and so do their families. After an ordination, church members often offer sympathy, rather than congratulations, to the chosen one and his family.

Church Sundays and Off Sundays

All Amish church services are long and intense. Most last three to four hours, followed by a noon meal and several hours of visiting. Due to the intensity of their worship, the Amish do not see the need to meet more than twice a month. Every other Sunday, one family opens its home to the congregation.

The Amish believe having a separate building for religious services is a waste of money. Meeting in

An Amish farmhouse in Lancaster County, Pennsylvania, stands next to two enormous silos.

homes brings communities closer. Once a year, each family knows its home and lifestyle will be on display for the congregation. How well they obey the Ordnung will be visible to anyone attending.

On the off Sunday, when there is no service, Amish families rest. Some travel to other districts to attend neighbor's services. Others read the *Bible* or tell their children stories. Sunday is a sacred day, so work is kept to a minimum.

Preparing for a Typical Church Sunday

Days ahead of the service, women begin preparing. They clean the entire house, since every room will be used—downstairs for the service and meal and upstairs for child care and resting. They prepare food for the noon meal. They sometimes bake pies, but more often they prepare simple foods, such as freshly baked breads, jams, butter, cheese, pickles, and sliced meats. As many as 200 people may attend the service.

Men and boys get the homestead ready for the coming crowd. They clean stables for their visitors' horses and set up backless wooden benches to seat everyone. Benches, hymnals, and eating utensils are stored in a special bench wagon, moved from home to home between services. Benches are arranged in close rows in the living room and other downstairs rooms, with a row of chairs at the front for men who conduct the service. In some cases, during good weather, benches are set up outdoors or in a barn or other outbuilding.

Amish Mennonite women bake pies in preparation for the noon meal after a church service.

The Preaching Service

On the day of the service, families get up earlier than usual to perform daily chores associated with farm life. After chores and breakfast, they harness horses to the buggy to travel to the home selected for that day's service. While people arrive, there is a period of visiting, with men near the barn, children clustered around the house, and women gathered in the kitchen.

When it is time to start the service, the Ordnung dictates the correct order for entering the home. Older, ordained men enter first, followed by other men, then women, and finally children, grouped by age and gender. During the service, men sit in the living room with their sons. Women sit in the kitchen or a downstairs bedroom with their daughters. Men conducting the service stand in the doorway so everyone can see. Infants are taken upstairs so they will not disrupt the solemn service.

Services are conducted in a mixture of languages—German, Pennsylvania Dutch, and English. Scriptures, however, are always read in German, and hymns sung in German. Many Amish congregations begin by singing hymns for almost an hour from the *Ausbund, das ist: Etliche schöne christliche Lieder*, or *An Excellent Selection of*

An Amish girl milks cows and performs other chores earlier than usual in order to attend an early morning service.

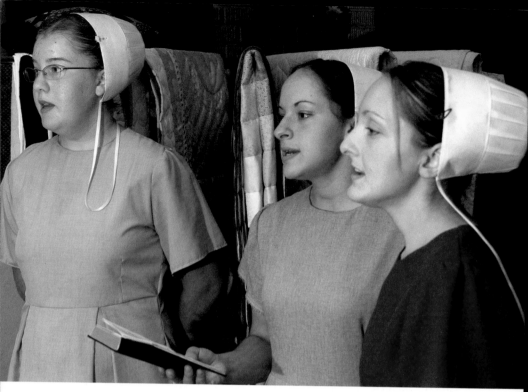

Amish women sing hymns, a very important part of the Amish church service.

Some Beautiful Christian Songs, their hymnal, first published in 1564 in Europe. The second hymn is always *Lob Lied,* meaning "Praise Song," which thanks God and asks that the ministers find the right words to preach.

Musical instruments are considered unnecessary. Choirs are likewise not allowed, because special singing inevitably leads some to focus on the quality of the song, or the abilities of the singer, rather than on the song's words. Amish singing is very slow, in unison, and resembles chanting rather than singing. To the Amish, the words, not the tune, are important.

After singing, the bishop or one of the ministers begins preaching. He begins by saying how unworthy he considers himself to preach, but that he will continue, since it is God's will. He quotes scripture from memory, tells *Bible* stories, and encourages members to be obedient and humble and to live pure lives. Ministers never prepare sermons in advance, which would be vain. During the service, several men speak, reading from the *Bible*, giving testimony, commenting on what the minister has said, or disagreeing with the sermon's message. Women never speak during a service.

Between the sermons and *Bible* readings, there are several periods of silence. Members stand, turn, and kneel for silent prayer. Often, congregations remain kneeling during the next scripture reading or while a minister reads a long prayer from a prayer book. The service usually ends with a closing hymn and sometimes announcements, such as the location of the next service.

The Noon Meal and Visiting Time

After the service, benches are rearranged, food is set out, and members eat together. Older members eat first. Children wait until the adults have finished. After lunch, children play, young people gather in groups to talk or go for walks, and adults visit.

At about 3:00 P.M., men hitch their buggies to take their families home or to neighbors' homes to continue visiting. Later in the afternoon, teenagers return to the farm where the service was held to socialize with their own age group. They spend the evening singing gospel songs a bit livelier than those sung during the morning service, or they pair off for supervised courting until about 10:00 P.M., when they escort their dates home.

CHAPTER FOUR

What Holidays Do I Celebrate?

The Amish celebrate most Christian holidays, including Christmas. They spend holidays praying, contemplating scriptures, and sometimes fasting (going without food). At Christmas, Amish families serve a feast and they exchange handmade greeting cards and gifts. The main difference is in the simplicity of the celebration.

In addition to religious holidays, the Amish hold special services twice each year to commemorate Holy Communion. Two additional special meetings, the Bishops' Meeting and the Counsel Meeting, are held in the weeks before communion to prepare the congregation spiritually. Special services are also held for baptisms and ordinations. The Amish also celebrate Thanksgiving.

Thanksgiving and Christmas

An Amish Thanksgiving usually begins with a family devotional. Each member tells what he or she thanks

An Amish Mennonite family in Tennessee gathers in their living room to pray on Christmas morning.

God for. Adults and older children spend the morning fasting and praying. In the evening, most Amish families enjoy a traditional Thanksgiving dinner, followed by visiting, fun, and games.

Like Thanksgiving Day, Christmas Day begins with devotionals and prayer. The Amish value simplicity and focus on the religious significance of the holiday, so children expect only one gift. They appreciate what they receive, knowing it came from their parents and not Santa Claus. On Christmas morning, gifts cannot be opened before the reading of the Gospel account of the birth of Jesus.

Many Amish families celebrate two Christmases—one solemn commemoration of Jesus's birth on December

25, and another, more joyful celebration on December 26, with family. Some conservative Amish groups commemorate January 6, known in Europe as the day of the Three Kings, a day of visiting and feasting.

Preparation for the Lord's Supper

Communion, the ritual based on Jesus's words at the Last Supper, is supremely meaningful for the Amish. Since they consider their church the body of Christ in the world, they must be pure to participate in the ritual. An Amish congregation will not hold communion unless every member agrees there are no unresolved disputes within the church and that everyone agrees with church rules. A congregation would rather skip communion than have it when they feel unprepared or unworthy. To become worthy, each congregation prepares itself through self-examination, confession, and cleansing, which requires several meetings.

The first, the Bishops' Meeting, is held several weeks before a scheduled communion, in March and again in September. Local bishops meet to discuss area problems, controversies concerning new technology, and obedience to the Ordnung.

Some issues bishops may discuss include whether it is acceptable for an Amish person to use a computer and go onto the Internet if that person's employer requires it. What about the use of cell phones? Can electricity be used on a farm if it is generated there, either by solar panels or through wind power, or should it still be prohibited because of its possible use to power a

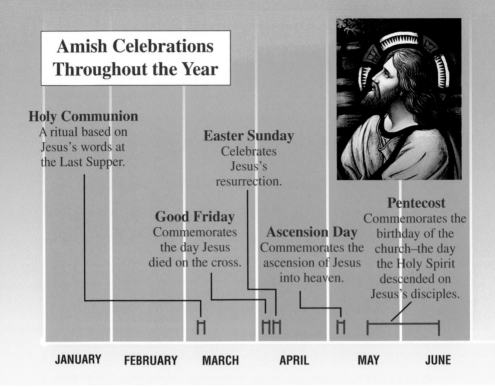

Amish Celebrations Throughout the Year

Holy Communion
A ritual based on Jesus's words at the Last Supper.

Easter Sunday
Celebrates Jesus's resurrection.

Good Friday
Commemorates the day Jesus died on the cross.

Ascension Day
Commemorates the ascension of Jesus into heaven.

Pentecost
Commemorates the birthday of the church–the day the Holy Spirit descended on Jesus's disciples.

JANUARY   FEBRUARY   MARCH   APRIL   MAY   JUNE

television, radio, or CD player? If the bishops agree on policy, it becomes part of the Ordnung.

Taking the Voice of the Church

Two weeks before communion, the entire membership holds a daylong meeting—part worship and part church business meeting. This is a **Counsel** Meeting, not a Council Meeting. In these meetings, members offer advice and counsel each other. They listen to sermons from the Old Testament about Abraham, Moses, and the deliverance of the Israelites from slavery. Ministers use these stories to reinforce the message that God's commands should be followed.

Following the preaching, the bishop recites the Ordnung and reports any changes that have been approved at the Bishops' Meeting. He asks members if all agree

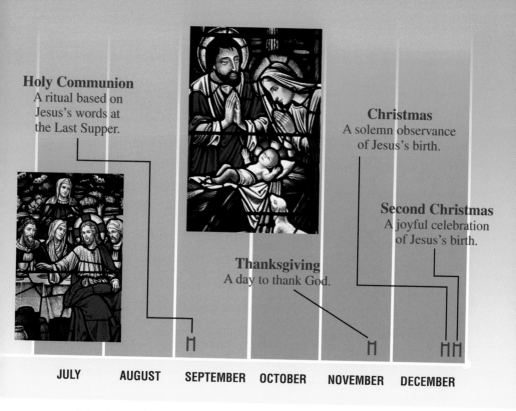

Holy Communion
A ritual based on
Jesus's words at
the Last Supper.

Christmas
A solemn observance
of Jesus's birth.

Second Christmas
A joyful celebration
of Jesus's birth.

Thanksgiving
A day to thank God.

JULY   AUGUST   SEPTEMBER   OCTOBER   NOVEMBER   DECEMBER

with the rules and whether anything stands in the way of their participation in the Lord's Supper. Church members sometimes confess their sins and ask forgiveness.

Finally, two ministers walk through the congregation and ask each member if they agree the congregation is ready. This is called "taking the voice of the church." If a member does not agree, he or she must explain the disagreement. Only when the church is in harmony can the communion service proceed.

One final step takes place on the Sunday before the communion service—the off Sunday. On that morning, church members fast, pray, and contemplate their readiness for the ceremony. Since Amish communion is only for members, only those baptized into the Amish Church can attend. Children who have not yet been baptized are not allowed at the service.

Communion Service

The communion service begins around 8:00 A.M., and continues until around 4:00 P.M. The first sermons generally begin with Genesis and retell stories of the Old Testament, focusing on stories that foretell the birth of Jesus. The second, much longer sermon, tells the life story of Jesus, ending with his suffering on the cross. At this point, a loaf of homemade bread and a cup of homemade wine are brought into the room. In turn, the bishop gives each member a piece of bread and a sip of wine—men first, then women.

After the Lord's Supper, buckets of water, washbasins, and towels are brought into the room. While

Amish children who have not yet been baptized are not allowed to participate in the communion service.

the congregation sings hymns, members take turns sitting in front of a basin, removing their shoes and socks, and allowing another member to wash and dry their feet. Men wash other men's feet, and women wash other women's feet.

When each pair has finished, they shake hands and exchange what is called a holy kiss, a kiss on the mouth between people of the same gender mentioned in 1 Corinthians 16:20. Once everyone has participated, the service is over, and everyone files out. At this service only, a deacon stands at the door to collect funds for the poor. No collection is taken at any other Amish service.

As peaceful and harmonious as the Amish seem to outsiders, there are still controversies and problems. Over the years, some members have wanted to relax the rules of the Ordnung, most often those about clothing, the construction of churches, the use of electricity, and whether Amish children should be educated past the eighth grade. Most Amish students are taught only the basic skills they need to farm and maintain Amish households. A high school or college education is considered unnecessary and would expose them to worldly values.

There are also occasional instances of physical and mental abuse, depression, and juvenile delinquency. The Amish deal with these problems in their own way, usually without outside interference. When bishops or ministers become aware of an abusive parent, they sometimes counsel families to treat each other with love, as Jesus taught. Amish publications, such as *Family Life*, encourage families by providing parenting tips in articles such as "Guidelines for Parents," "Anger! Danger Zone," and "Being Worthy of Your Child's Respect." Despite their separation from outsiders, though, Amish victims of abuse sometimes seek help from doctors and family counselors.

Economic pressures have led some Amish groups to compromise with the outside world. In many communities, Amish men and women work outside the home and off the farm. Some own and operate their own stores, usually antique shops, quilt or craft shops, bakeries, or farmers' markets, selling to their own people and to tourists. Some, like Amish furniture makers,

A classroom of Amish Mennonite children listen attentively to their teacher. Most Amish children do not attend school past the eighth grade.

An Amish woman in Florida sells fruit from a roadside stand outside her community.

have outgrown their communities, supplying their products to national stores such as Wal-Mart.

Today, the Amish are thriving despite internal conflict, further splits within the Amish church (as recently as 1966), and changes caused by outside pressure. Their population continues to grow due to large family size and because a large number of children choose the security and comfort of their parents' religion.

The Amish today live much as their ancestors have lived since the foundation of their faith in 1525. Through discipline, strong will, and a stubborn sense of tradition, they maintain what seems to be a simple, stress-free lifestyle in a rapidly changing world, but even they cannot escape all the stresses of family life.

GLOSSARY

banned: Forbidden.

baptize: To pour water on someone's head or immerse them in water as a sign that he or she has become a Christian or has joined a particular church.

communion: A Christian service in which people eat bread and drink wine or grape juice to remember the last meal of Jesus.

conform: To behave in the same way as everyone else in a particular group or to behave in a way that is expected of you.

conservative: Moderate, cautious; someone who opposes radical change and likes things to stay as they are or used to be.

counsel: To listen to people's problems and give advice.

excommunicated: Officially excluded from participating in religious services, particularly communion; having church membership revoked.

ordination: A ceremony that brings someone into the priesthood or the ministry.

salvation: The state of being saved from sin, evil, harm, or destruction.

scripture: A sacred book or passages from a sacred book.

sect: A group whose members share the same beliefs and practices or follow the same leader. A sect is often a religious group that has broken away from a larger church.

shunning: The act of avoiding someone or something on purpose.

FOR FURTHER EXPLORATION

Books

Richard Ammon, *Amish Christmas*. New York: Simon & Schuster Children's, 2000. A Christmas without Santa Claus? It is possible! Warm pastel illustrations show how the Amish celebrate Christmas.

———, *An Amish Year*. New York: Atheneum Books for Young Readers, 2000. An Amish girl describes a year in her life, including social customs, and lifestyle. Includes color photographs.

Raymond Bial, *Amish Home*. Boston: Houghton Mifflin, 1993. Discusses the way of life of the Amish, using color photography and clear text.

Doris Faber, *Amish*. New York: Doubleday, 1991. Traces the European roots of the Amish, and discusses their philosophy and beliefs and the issues facing the Amish today.

Phyllis Pellman Good, *Amish Children*. Intercourse, PA: Good Books, 2000. Unforgettable photographs and thoughtful text concerning growing up Amish. Covers such topics as "Going to School," "Learning to Work," and "Joining the Church."

John A. Hostetler, *Amish Life*. Lancaster, PA: Herald Press, 1989. An authoritative introduction to the Amish—their lifestyle, beliefs, social institutions, and customs.

Dewayne E. Pickles and Fred L. Israel, *Amish*. Langhorne, PA: Chelsea House, 1995. Relates the history of the Amish and their religious beliefs, practices, rites, and ceremonies.

Peggy Fletcher Stack, *A World of Faith*. Salt Lake City, UT: Signature, 2001. An overview of 28 world faiths, including the Amish. Handsome and informative, with simple, straightforward text and beautiful illustrations. An excellent springboard for further study.

Louise Stoltzfus, *Amish Women*. Intercourse, PA: Good Books, 1997. The author recounts her life growing up Amish. Includes interviews with ten Amish women.

Katherine Wagner, *Life in an Amish Community*. San Diego, CA: Lucent, 2001. Somewhat advanced for young readers, but an excellent resource. Covers such topics as marriage, education, religion, getting along with outsiders, and more. Quotations from primary sources, annotated bibliography, and black-and-white photographs.

Jean Kinney Williams, *The Amish*. New York: Scholastic, 1996. Discusses the history, beliefs, practices, social structure, and modern problems of the Amish.

Periodicals

These periodicals focus on Amish life and can be obtained from the addresses below.

Family Life. LaGrange, IN, 46761

Young Companion Pathway. LaGrange, IN, 46761

Videos

The Amish: A People of Preservation. VHS. Written and produced by John L. Ruth. A Heritage Production. Worcester, PA: Gateway Films/Vision Video, 1991. Introduces various aspects of Amish life—their customs, history, basic beliefs, and lifestyle. Filmed in Lancaster County, Pennsylvania.

Devil's Playground. DVD. Directed by Lucy Walker. Produced by Steven Cantor. Wellspring, in association with Stick Figure Productions, Cinemax Reel Life, and Channel Four. Wellspring, 2002. A look at the Amish tradition of rumspringa, a time for teenagers to run wild before choosing to become baptized members of the Amish Church.

Web Sites

The Amish & the Plain People (www.800padutch.com/amish.shtml). A site run by the Pennsylvania Dutch Welcome Center, providing in-depth information about the Amish.

Amish Country (www.billybear4kids.com/Amish/fun.html). A children's site providing access to an Amish storybook, jigsaw puzzles, coloring book pages, paper dolls, and recipes. Some items on the site must be downloaded and require a small fee.

National Committee for Amish Religious Freedom (www.holycrosslivonia.org/amish). The history of the Amish and frequently asked questions about the Amish.

The People's Place (www.thepeoplesplace.com). A tourist site dedicated to the Pennsylvania Dutch region of Pennsylvania and the Amish culture.

INDEX

PICTURE CREDITS

ABOUT THE AUTHOR

Charles George taught history and Spanish in Texas public schools for sixteen years. He lives with his wife of 34 years, Linda, in West Texas. Together, they have written over 50 young adult and children's nonfiction books. Charles has written two Lucent books, *Life Under the Jim Crow Laws* and *Civil Rights*. For KidHaven, he has written *The Holocaust*, part of the History of the World series, and *What Makes Me A Buddhist?*, *What Makes Me A Hindu?*, and *What Makes Me A Mormon?* for the series What Makes Me A . . . ? He and Linda also wrote *Texas* for the Seeds of a Nation series.